Class 37s in the Far West

Class 37s in the Far West

STEPHEN C MARSHALL and ROGER GEACH

© Roger Geach, 2019

Published by Budleigh

A CIP catalogue record for this book is available from the British Library.

ISBN 978-0-9955665-1-4

Book layout and cover design by Clare Brayshaw

Front cover photograph – Mid-afternoon at the picturesque location of Golant finds the tide in as 37673 is passing with export clay bound for Carne Point, Fowey 12th April 1995. At this time the locomotive had no decals and was recently repainted in Railfreight Grey – *Photo R. Geach*

Back cover photograph – An amazing sight in The Duchy in the new millennium was large logo blue liveried 37425 which spent two days working off St Blazey at the end of May 2005. This was a full four years after their displacement by the Class 66s. Here 37425 of Cardiff Canton takes a break from it's almost daily use on the Cardiff to Rhymney passenger turns to work 6B26 1355 from Burngullow Jn to St Blazey yard passing St Austell.

Frontispiece – 37175 heads west through Newton Abbot with ball clay from Heathfield on 8th August 1986. The diesel depot had by this time been closed for around six years and evidence of track removal can be seen on the right of the picture, together with the long disused washing plant – *Photo S. Crowther*

Prepared by:

York Publishing Services Ltd
64 Hallfield Road
Layerthorpe
York YO31 7ZQ

Tel: 01904 431213

Website: www.yps-publishing.co.uk

Contents

Personal Introduction

I am standing on the stone bridge at Lavrean on the Par to Newquay branch line. For those who are not familiar with the area, Lavrean is the Par side of Goonbarrow Junction where a minor road crosses the railway and where one could see the semaphore distant signal for Goonbarrow Junction. The weather is cold but with sunny spells and there is a heightened expectancy of something exciting about to happen. So, we wait and wait. Today is the first run of a class 37 into Cornwall and our good friends at Plymouth Laira depot have advised us that 37142 their new arrival will be making its very first trip out for crew training purposes from Plymouth to Goonbarrow junction. Alas after much waiting nothing has arrived, so I head back towards Bodmin and Liskeard wondering if the trip has been cancelled or run only as far as Par. The information was that the training trip will return from Par behind the up Cornish Rivera, the 1055 from Penzance to Paddington due off Liskeard at 1217. 50036 departs Liskeard on time so once again we wait to see if anything will follow. The sun is still out. There is nothing now due on the up until 1354. Low and behold at 1234 the up-road signals come off, so we now hope that this may be the training trip. Sure enough at 1240 the unmistakable snout of a 37 pokes its nose around the corner and makes a leisurely approach to Liskeard with a rake of grampus wagons behind it complete with brake van. I record the scene for posterity taking one more going away shot as it heads through the station and away back towards Plymouth. What a moment to savour a new type of locomotive in the county. My wife is not impressed at all, as I am late back having been missing all morning.

However, it was a very small moment in history and I can look back on that day with happy memories; it's not often you get to see and photograph a new type of locomotive in Cornwall on its first trip.

A historic picture of 37142 returning to Plymouth Laira with the first crew training run into Cornwall on the 9th February 1978 seen passing Liskeard Station – *Photo R Geach*

37142 is seen stabled by the old daily shed and sand house at Plymouth Laira depot on 9th February 1978 – *Photo R Geach*

About the Authors

ROGER GEACH

Roger was born and brought up in Liskeard, East Cornwall.

Being a West-Country boy he grew up with the diesel-hydraulics and naturally they made a huge impression on him. He witnessed the demise of the hydraulics, but his regular visits to South Wales produced sightings of numerous work-stained and grubby diesel-electrics, which were then known simply as English Electric type 3s.

These type 3s were subsequently classified as Class 37, and Roger found that photography, particularly of freight, became his main interest. A subsequent move to Hertfordshire resulted in these interesting machines working on his doorstep and thus his interest in this particular class of diesel was heightened.

STEPHEN C MARSHALL

Steve, as he is known, grew up in Manchester but left there to move to Paignton in Devon with his family in 1962, aged 12.

His railway interest had emerged when he was 8 years old and thus he witnessed the introduction of many of the first generation diesels, sharing duties with steam locomotives. However the move to Devon in 1962 just about coincided with the end of steam in that part of the country and all main line diesel types were solely diesel-hydraulic.

Like most enthusiasts, he grew up as a spotter, but managed to 'clear his books' by 1972 and further challenges were needed. Thus he then set about acquiring haulage behind as many different locomotives, of all types, as possible, his earliest Class 37 hauled journey being as long ago as August 1967 when D6709, D6744, D6794 and D6803 were all encountered during an all-line railrover.

Photography was always important, later accompanied by videoing as the added dimension of sound was appealing.

He still retains his interest to this day and can be seen at some of the railway galas or even travelling on the big railway he first encountered all those years ago.

Roger and Steve decided to collaborate to produce this book in order to record the history of the Class 37s in the West Country. Steve's record keeping and Roger's photographic collection enabled this to be done.

Acknowledgements

The majority of the photographs in this book are our own, Roger Geach and Stephen C. Marshall. Coverage is much enhanced by using the following friends' photographs. Bernard Mills based at Plymouth, Colin Moss from the West Midlands who holidayed regularly in Cornwall. Nigel Ward who has scanned and helped Colin with his pictures. Steve Woodbridge and Philip Gardner from Paignton, Steve Crowther, Stuart O'Dell and Michael Rowe, all from around Newton Abbot. Robin Fell who kindly let me look through the Transport Treasury Collection based at High Wycombe.

We should like to thank the following friends and enthusiasts in no particular order who provided and confirmed the information which has helped to build up the data base of class 37 passenger workings.

Philip Bolton, Adrian Noel, Graham Braund, Matthew Burridge, Andrew Butler, Philip Butler, the late Barry Bastin, Alan Tait, Alistair Tait, Dean Stanley, Mick Parker, David Rickett, the late John Mellor, Nick Edwards, the late John Frood, Sean Greenslade, Lloyd Guppy, David Keogh, Cyril Lord, Craig Munday, Tony Shore, Pip Dunn, Andrew Pearce, Nick Perring, Jez Darr, David Barraclough, Chris Pelling, Steve Hale, Steve Radford, Michael Hayes, Mike Turner, Charles Woodland, A.Davies, L.Hart, P.Webber, J. Powell.

The following groups along with their Web Sites

      The Cornwall Railway Society

      The Growler Group

      The Plymouth Railway Circle

      Class 37.co.uk for information on the history of the locomotives

      Six Bells Junction Website for information regarding Railtours.

Also John Vaughan for answering queries on all matters Cornish. Michael Mercer for allocations and class 37 information. Thanks to all.

Introduction

Welcome to our book on the Class 37s in the West Country. For the purposes of this book, we have defined the West Country as any lines west of Taunton on the Paddington & Bristol to Penzance route of the former Western Region, and West of Yeovil Junction on the Waterloo to Exeter St Davids former London & South Western route.

The main part of the book will look at the period from 1978 when the class 37s arrived at Plymouth Laira depot to be outbased at St Blazey in Cornwall.

The Class 37, although a mixed traffic engine, was very much a freight locomotive. Some examples had boilers for steam heat and could be used on passenger services. However, they were not diagrammed for any passenger work in the West Country and the opportunity to see them on passenger services in this area was normally one of pure luck.

We also include a database of all known Class 37 passenger workings in our area. Such a listing can never be 100% complete as we learn about previously unreported workings from the internet and other enthusiasts as time goes by. We will continue to record new workings as they are discovered. A particularly difficult area is Cornwall, where the reports and observations were more spasmodic than around Exeter and Newton Abbot. The database is shown at the end of Chapter 6 and covers the years from 1965 to 2004.

Class 37s covered failures by other locomotives and assisted High Speed Trains when in difficulty but interestingly there were no diagrammed passenger trains in the South West, unlike many parts of the country.

We will look at their work in the South West, which was primarily for freight duties, particularly clay traffic. We also list the allocations of West Country based 37s from 1978 to 1993.

Railtours from 1977 are also included and listed in a separate chapter. These trains brought the class to some of the branch lines such as St Ives and Looe. This gave a unique opportunity to ride behind these engines on a route that rarely saw locomotive hauled trains.

The Class 37s arrived in 1978, quite late to the far West, unlike many other areas. They were good workhorses and whether you watched from the lineside or rode behind them they were reliable locomotives. On a cold still frosty evening in winter one could hear them far away when climbing the Fowey (or Glynn) Valley from Bodmin Road up to Liskeard with a heavy freight. The locomotives were generally liked by local railway staff and enthusiasts. We hope you enjoy our book.

Chapter 1 – Early Days

Some readers may not know that Class 37s made occasional sorties west of Bristol in the early 1970s.

They were rare and one had to be extremely lucky to see one, particularly west of Taunton. The nearest depot with any trained drivers was Bristol Bath Road.

Pairs of 37s were used on the Aberthaw to Highbridge pulverised fly ash trains during 1970 and 1971. This was waste material from Aberthaw Power Station near Barry in South Wales and was used during the construction of the M5 motorway in Somerset.

A clean blue 6957 is seen in multiple with 6607 working a flyash train from Aberthaw to Highbridge, standing at Bristol Temple Meads on the 16th August 1971. This was the nearest that a class 37 ventured into the West Country at this time – *Photo R. Geach*

Further, on Wednesday 31st May 1972 a green 6923 arrived at Exeter St Davids with the afternoon 1553 Bristol to Plymouth van train 4B10. It was removed on arrival and went straight back to Bristol light loco, with class 42 Warship 832 Onslaught taking over the train to Plymouth. I was on the station at Exeter St Davids that day and was very surprised to see this appear.

Green liveried with full yellow ends 6923 has surprisingly arrived at Exeter St Davids with the 4B10 1553 Bristol Temple Meads to Plymouth parcel service on the 31st May 1972. Here it was removed. 6923 returned light locomotive to Bristol immediately – *Photo R. Geach*

The open day at Laira depot on Saturday 23rd September 1972 provided the opportunity to view a clean 6997 which had hauled steam loco 6000 King George V down from Hereford to the open day for display.

No records were found showing any visit by a Class 37 to the West Country during 1973.

On the 29 January 1974 37220 worked one of the sugar beet services into Exeter Riverside yard. In those days there were plenty of sugar beet specials that ran seasonally originating from various locations in East Anglia.

During February and March 1974 the wheel lathe at Cardiff Canton was out of action for a short period. This meant that any class 37s that required tyre turning were sent to Plymouth Laira depot, normally in pairs. The first visit for tyre turning that we know of took place on the 22nd February 1974 when 6930 was seen at 1433 hours on a 9Z04 freight at Exeter. Sean Greenslade worked at Exeter St Davids at this time in the telegraph office as it was then, and he kept a look out for anything unusual. Exact details of train 9Z04 are not clear.

Just three days later on the 25th February 1974, TOPS renumbered 37292 (ex-6992), together with 6922 were seen at Exeter heading light locos from Laira depot back to South Wales at 1820 hrs after tyre turning. Further observations of Class 37 visits for tyre turning were as follows. On the 4th March 1974 6934+6896 passed Exeter at 1601 hrs returning to Bristol. On 6th March 1974 37269+37299 were noted at Exeter travelling towards Plymouth at 1653, 37269 being noted at Laira on 15th March 74.

On the 8th March 1974 D1014 Western Leviathan and 37272 were observed heading towards Plymouth at 1534 hours and on the 11th March 1974 37272+37299 were noted passing Exeter at 1537 returning from Plymouth to Bristol. The Cardiff wheel lathe must have been back in action soon afterwards as no further 37s were seen in transit after this date.

37308 worked 7B33 1130 Severn Tunnel Junction to Exeter Riverside freight on the 29 March 1974.

37272 is seen on the Wheel Lathe at Plymouth Laira depot Sunday 10th March 1974. For a short period of time tyre turning was carried out on these locomotives at Plymouth due to the Cardiff Canton lathe being out of action – *Photo R. Geach*

On the 14th May 1974 37142 arrived at Exeter with 6B36 1225 Avonmouth to Exeter City basin tanks. It returned to Bristol light loco at 1605 hrs. Just under a month later on the 13th June 1974 37299 worked 6B36 and once again returned light loco late afternoon.

The next recorded freight working was on the 18th June 1974 and was Eastern Region based 37168 with the weed killer train. This was a 6Z11 0655 Langwith Junction (near Shirebrook) to Exeter South Devon sidings arriving at 2019 hrs, returning light loco almost immediately. 37168 was based at Thornaby depot in the North East at that time and was a very rare loco to be seen that far west. On the 25th July 1974 37221 worked the 7B34 Bristol Kingsland Road to Redruth Drump Lane freight as far as Exeter Riverside Yard.

It was not then until the 4th September 1974 that a 37 was seen again at Exeter when 37224 arrived with the 6B36 1225 Avonmouth to Exeter City Basin tanks.

The next observation was on the 8th October 1974 when 37235 was seen in ex works condition on Exeter stabling point at 1345 hours with the headcode 7B14 displayed. The actual working is not known.

On the 30th October 37303 arrived, once again with the 6B36 1225 Avonmouth to Exeter City Basin oil, and the 14th November brought 37240 with the 6B09 1840 Swindon to Exeter Riverside empty milk tanks. It returned on the 0025 Exeter Riverside to Avonmouth freight.

1975 brought only two confirmed observations for class 37s at Exeter. The first was on the 1st April 1975 when 37208+37293 arrived with the 6B36 1225 Avonmouth – Exeter City Basin oil, while 37138 was observed on the stabling point at 1612 hrs with 8B32 displayed in the head code panel.

1976 produced one famous passenger duty that we shall look at later, but there were no further freight observations until 1977 when on the 29th October 37232 hauled 46006 light to Exeter. The years from 1978 onward are covered in another chapter.

Chapter 2 – Class 37 allocations to Plymouth Laira depot by year

1978	WEF
37142	5-2-1978
37267	19-2-1978

1980	
37299	01/1980
37206	10/1980
37274	10/1980

1981	
37207	10/1981

1982	
37181	3-10-1982
37182	3-10 -982

1983	
37185	17-4-1983
37270	17-4-1983
37272	17-4-1983

1984	
37247	13-5-1984

1985	
37196	11-2-1985
37222	12-8-1985

1986	
37235	2-2-1986
37175	11-5-1986

1987	
37670	(ex 37182) 12-4-87
37671	(ex 37247) 5-4-87
37672	(ex 37189) 5-4-87
37673	(ex 37132) 5-4-87
37674	(ex 37169) 5-4-87
37675	(ex 37164) 12-4-87

1989	
37412	19-2-1989
37414	14-5-1989
37669	1-1-1989

1990	
37411	30-9-1990
37413	10/1990

1991	
37417	10-3-1991
37420	10-3-1991

1993	
37416	23-5-1993
37521	12-12-1993
37668	12-12-1993

Chapter 3 – The First Arrival

37142 was the first Class 37 allocated to work in the West Country and based at Plymouth Laira. The intention was to replace the Class 25 locos, though this turned out to be a slow process and the last 25s were not finally displaced until autumn 1980.

Class 37 37142 was reallocated from Swansea Landore to Plymouth Laira depot on 5th February 1978, though it's precise arrival date in Devon is unrecorded.

However, history was made on Thursday 9th February 1978 when it worked into Cornwall with a crew training special conveying a rake of open trucks for handling purposes.

This was the very first working of a class 37 into Cornwall as advised by our friends at Laira depot. The loco and wagons returned to Tavistock Junction behind the up Penzance to Paddington service seen passing Liskeard at 1240 hours on that day. At 5pm that afternoon 37142 was observed back at Laira depot. Crew training continued until the last week of February with the loco normally working down behind the 0840 Plymouth to Penzance service to Par and returning behind the 1055 Penzance to Paddington service.

D6842 (TOPS number 37142) was new to traffic from 17th May 1963 having been built at the Vulcan Foundry, Newton Le Willows, Lancashire. D6842 was very much a freight locomotive and was not built with a train heating boiler for passenger use. First allocated to Cardiff Canton it was a South Wales freight engine until transferred to Glasgow Polmadie depot in August 1966. It remained based in Scotland and after a short stay at Eastfield depot it moved to Landore depot, Swansea from November 1972. D6842 was renumbered into the BR TOPS system at some point during March 1974. 37142 continued to work from its South Wales depot until it transferred to Plymouth Laira depot on 5th February 1978.

37142 remained a Plymouth based locomotive until the 17th April 1983 when it was moved away to Cardiff Canton and its association with St Blazey finished. However it was seen back in the West Country, including St Blazey at times, when based at Canton as a Regional Railways South Wales and West locomotive, or Trainload Freight West 37/0 also based at Canton. Unlike many class 37s, 37142 was never converted or refurbished and it retained its guise until it was withdrawn from service. 37142 was one of a small number that received a general overhaul at Plymouth Laira depot arriving during December 1989 and not departing until February 1990. It was painted into departmental grey with black numbers. This was at the time when more locomotive overhauls were carried out at the larger level 5 depots rather than sending them to the BREL works. The locomotive history shows that it was stored unserviceable from 1st May 1997. At that time the locomotive was based at Crewe Diesel depot. EWS disposed of the locomotive and after a short period at Barrow Hill it was purchased by the Bodmin & Wenford Diesel Group in May 2003, heading to their Bodmin base in September of that year; finally returning to Cornwall. The locomotive ran for the first time in preservation on 25th August 2004 and has now spent longer based at Bodmin in preservation that at any BR depot during its operating life.

During its BR ownership the loco carried various liveries. Delivered in BR green with small yellow panels, it was later repainted blue with full yellow ends. It also had a period in BR Civil livery, all over grey with yellow ends, and was then painted into what was known as Dutch livery; described as such because many Dutch locomotives were painted in similar colours. This was a grey lower side body with all over yellow upper half and full yellow ends. It was withdrawn from service in this livery after 34 years in service.

A well work worn 37142 is seen shunting a syphon G parcel van onto a parcel train in the up platform at Swindon 6th March 1976. It would appear the van has just been overhauled at Swindon Works as it is sparkling clean. Note the headcode still displays 9Z10, although the need to display headcode on locos had been abolished from January of that year – *Photo S.C. Marshall*

37142 is seen passing Cardiff Canton on an automotive service loaded with new Ford Cars . The headcode box at this end is now wound to show four zeros. 22nd May 1976 – *Photo S.C. Marshall*

37142 together with 37304 and 37301, is rather unusually found leading the Llanwern to Port Talbot iron ore empties past Cardiff Canton depot on the 25th November 1976. This was a regular triple headed working but normally only locos with specially strengthened couplings were used. These were primarily the higher numbered locomotives in the class – *Photo S.C. Marshall*

37142 arrives at Par with refurbished milk tanks for St Blazey yard. These milk tanks saw very limited use as the Milk Marketing board had changed its transport requirements. Summer 1980 – *Photo Transport Treasury*

37142 is passing Bristol Temple Meads on the 3rd July 1987 with a domestic coal service from Radyr to Exmouth Junction – *Photo R. Geach*

37142 recently ex works with new paintwork is stabled at Newport Godfrey Road on the 4th June 1988. Amongst other 37s stabled on the shed are 37263, 37207 and 37146 – *Photo R. Geach*

Dutch liveried 37142, by now a Cardiff Canton loco, is seen at Beam Bridge, on the east side of Whiteball tunnel and approaching Wellington, with oil empties from Heathfield to Waterston, West Wales on 3rd March 1992 – *Photo S. Crowther*

37142 is now part of the heritage fleet based at the Bodmin & Wenford Railway in Cornwall. On the 7th October 2018 it is seen at Charlies Gate, soon after departing Bodmin Parkway, heading for Bodmin General – *Photo R. Geach*

Chapter 4 – Freight Duties in the South West

All of the Plymouth Laira allocated class 37s were outbased at St Blazey depot in mid-Cornwall, primarily for the china clay traffic. Prior to the arrival of these type 3s the locally based china clay workings had been in the hands of the Sulzer class 25 locomotives which arrived during the summer of 1971 to replace the North British class 22 locomotives. For just under two years from Feb 1978 until the autumn of 1980 both 37s and 25s worked alongside each other.

St Blazey depot was built by the Cornish Minerals Railway as its headquarters and opened in 1874. This was a half roundhouse of nine covered roads served by a turntable. There were also various offices and a wagon repair shed. The half roundhouse survived into the class 37 era and was in use until April 1987. It was then converted for industrial use. The turntable survives to the present day and was used to turn class 37 locos in order to even out wheel flange wear. The old wagon repair shops were modernized to accommodate locomotive servicing along with a new fuel point from April 1987.

Easter 1987, and 37196, "Tre Pol and Pen" in the attractive red stripe Railfreight livery, and fitted with miniature snow ploughs, is seen on the turntable at St Blazey depot. It will be stabled in the roundhouse for the night. 37196 was very much a Cornish locomotive for over two years, arriving during February 1985, until it was transferred away to Cardiff Canton during July 1987 – *Photo C. Moss*

Swansea Landore locomotive 37307 is stabled on St Blazey depot by the old fuel point on the 23rd June 1984. Behind right can be seen part of the 1874 former Cornwall Minerals Railway buildings. There is also a DMU vehicle stabled – *Photo S.C. Marshall*

37193 of Thornaby depot is stabled at St Blazey on 12th August 1985 – *Photo C. Moss*

Another rare visitor is 37096, also a Thornaby locomotive, which had worked down to Plymouth on a York to Plymouth relief on 9th August 1984. It had made its way to St Blazey depot, seen on the evening of the 11th August 1984 – *Photo C. Moss*

Full house for the night. 37247 is stabled outside the shed, and left to right inside the roundhouse are 37273, a visitor from Cardiff Canton, local engines 37181, 37185 and Landore loco 37307. August 1984 – *Photo C. Moss*

37267 at Bodmin Road is about to shunt the loaded clay wagons from Wenfordbridge out onto the mainline and head off to Fowey. 26th July 1978 – *Photo R. Geach*

An intruder in the Duchy of Cornwall on 27th June 1990 is 37298 of Tinsley depot, unofficially named "Victor", and seen passing Bodmin Parkway with empty CDAs for Plymouth Marsh Mills. Note the red lines on the front of the loco, which refer to the 'V' as in 'Valley Lines' services operated by the local DMUs in the Cardiff area. This despite the loco not being South Wales based. Also, of interest is the class 52 D1048 Western Lady, stored in the sidings of the Bodmin & Wenford Steam Railway – *Photo S. Crowther*

37267 with empty clay hoods heads away from Lostwithiel at Milltown bound for Burngullow on the lovely afternoon of the 18th September 1978 – *Photo R. Geach*

Split headcode 37026, from Tinsley depot Sheffield, is seen departing Lostwithiel up loop with clay for Fowey on the 29th December 1993. No doubt covering temporarily for one of the local class 37s – *Photo R. Geach*

37299 arrives at Lostwithiel with a loaded clay train for Carne Point Fowey. It will run round in the loop north of the station. Note the track machine stabled in the old goods yard and the former broad gauge goods shed still standing. This area is all housing now. 22nd April 1980 – *Photo R. Geach*

37207 "William Cookworthy" arrives at Lostwithiel with loaded clay hoods for Fowey. It is passing the stone built former locomotive works of the Cornwall railway Company now a housing development. 37207 carries the Cornish Lizard symbol and Cornish Railways on the front of the locomotive. This was in the days when the Area Manager Truro controlled all activity within Cornwall. 22nd April 1987 – *Photo R. Geach*

37181 brings a rake of empty clay hoods off the Fowey Branch at Lostwithiel on Thursday 24th March 1983. 37181 was a regular locomotive working in Cornwall from October 1982 until August 1985 – *Photo R. Geach*

Lostwithiel was quite a busy location, where many of the clay trains would run round or shunt into the yard. Here 37206 departs from Lostwithiel on 28th January 1981 with clay hood empties. Note another rake in the down yard. 37206 arrived at Laira during October 1980 – *Photo B. Mills*

Wednesday 10th April 1985, and snow plough fitted 37247 powers up at Milltown with empty clay hoods from Fowey to Burngullow. 37247 carries the stencilled 'Cornish Railways' transfer on the side. 37247 spent two years based at Plymouth Laira from May 1984 to May1986 – *Photo R. Geach*

Refurbished 37670 is seen passing Coulson Park, Lostwithiel on the 3rd September 1987 with clay hoods for Fowey. Fully refurbished locomotives only worked the clay hoods for a short time as all the CDA wagons were in traffic by February 1988 – *Photo R. Geach*

37672, named "Freight Transport Association" runs alongside the River Fowey at Lostwithiel with clay bound for Fowey Docks on the 17th July 1991 – *Photo R. Geach*

Looking down the valley, large logo 37175 heads empty wagons alongside the River Fowey, seen from near to Milltown on the 22 April 1987 – *Photo R. Geach*

Golant, on the Fowey branch, is a classic location to photograph trains. Sunshine and a high tide were always a huge bonus if they coincided with the passing of a clay train.

Climbing one of the steep hills that surround the village, this view looking down towards the River Fowey became possible. 37196 is seen on 3rd September 1986 – *Photo R. Geach*

This is the low level view at Golant with the tide well and truly out. 37207 'William Cookworthy 'slows for the level crossing at Golant on 10th September 1986. 37207 was truly a Cornish engine, arriving in October 1981 and spending six years allocated to Plymouth Laira depot, almost all of which was spent working in Cornwall – *Photo R. Geach*

Railfreight Distribution liveried 37414 is seen at Golant with clay for Fowey on the 18th July 1990. 37414 spent only four months in the FCLL pool from May to September 1990 – *Photo R. Geach*

Cardiff Canton based 37281 at Treesmill, near Par, with empty clay hoods for St Blazey yard on 22nd March 1983. Note the numbers 281 stenciled on the locomotives' nose, a feature that appeared on several South Wales based class 37s – *Photo R. Geach*

A scruffy 37203 brings empty hoods into Par Station bound for Goonbarrow Junction. It was a Bristol Bath Road based locomotive at the time covering duties at St Blazey, and was a regular for a while in the summer of 1981 – *Photo Transport Treasury*

Another Bristol Bath Road engine working in Cornwall was 37135 on empty hoods from Fowey to Burngullow, seen approaching Par Station in lovely evening light on 4th September 1986 – *Photo R. Geach*

October 1981, and a yet to be named 37207 is seen at Par station with the afternoon mixed freight from Parkandillack, now heading for St Blazey yard. Note the flat-topped tarpaulin clay wagons which will be destined to travel out of the county later that evening – *Photo R. Geach*

The Newquay branch hosted dries at Ponts Mill, a large complex at Rocks situated at Goonbarrow Junction, on the Carbis branch near Bugle and the Retew branch to Meledor Mill. At Bodmin Road the former passenger route to Padstow remained open as a freight only line as far as Wadebridge. From Boscarne Junction the mineral line to Wenfordbridge was worked solely by Class 08 shunting locomotive to the dries situated there. A 37 would trip empties to Boscarne Junction and take loaded wagons back to Fowey. In the East of the County were the Moorswater dries on the Looe branch. A short line served this location from Coombe Junction.

37308, then based at Landore Swansea and the last of the class, is approaching Goonbarrow Junction with empty clayhoods for Rock dries on 5th September 1985 – *Photo R. Geach*

A view from Merthen Farm bridge looking back towards Carlyon Bay, and 37176 of Bristol Bath Road depot brings the morning clay trip from Drinnick Mill back to St Blazey. Notice the acid tank right behind the locomotive. 29th March 1984 – *Photo R. Geach*

37671, named "Tre Pol and Pen" and with red nameplates, passes Kernick with loaded CDA wagons from Parkandillack on the 6th September 1989 – *Photo R. Geach*

37674 departs from what was then, a rural Parkandillack, with a mixture of bogie wagons, which includes some PBA Tiger wagons. These will later form the service from St Blazey to Cliffe Vale. 3rd August 1993 – *Photo R. Geach*

In the heart of clay country taken from the Goonvean pit spoil tip near Slip Bridge, 37413 has just left Kernick with the afternoon mixed trip working. Among the train consist are bogie Tiger freight Polybulk and also CDA vehicles. 5th April 1993 – *Photo R. Geach*

37267 is seen near Foxhole with a rake of empty clay hoods for loading at Parkandillack in September 1978. Note the white waste material piled in conical heaps on the horizon. This was very much part of Clay Country in those days – *Photo R. Geach*

Moorswater clay works normally sent out one loaded train each day. In this view 37175 is seen at the entrance about to shunt some loaded wagons. 1st September 1986 – *Photo R. Geach*

37207, complete with snow ploughs, shunts at Moorswater clay works in 1981 – *Photo Transport Treasury*

In Devon, on the outskirts of Plymouth, was Marsh Mills served by a short branch from Tavistock Junction. This was only worked by diesel shunters, the 37 working to Tavistock Junction yard. Further east at Newton Abbot was the Heathfield branch with loading points at Heathfield and other locations on the branch. This was for loading ball clay slightly different to the china clay further west.

North Devon also loaded ball clay from the works at Petrockstowe and Meeth. Some of this was exported through the port of Fowey and would be worked down to Exeter by a Cass 31 or a 25 based at Exeter and then forward to Tavistock Junction yard, Plymouth or direct to Lostwithiel. Normally a Type 4 was used, but 37s did trip from Tavistock Junction to Fowey with the ball clay. Ball clay both loose and bagged was also sent to other destinations.

Local based 37247, complete with stenciled "Cornwall Railways" embellishment, is seen at Langford Bridge, Aller Junction, near Newton Abbot, with clay "hoods" from Heathfield to Fowey on the 9th March 1985 – *Transport Treasury*

The china clay industry went through many changes and in the early 1980s many loading points were closed. The Retew branch was in decline and traffic had dropped dramatically, with eventual closure coming in 1982 along with the North Devon lines to Meeth.

In 1978 there were only two Class 37 locos working from St Blazey. These were heavily utilised along with the still present class 25 locomotives. Naturally the training of fitters and drivers also had to be accommodated into the schedules. One might find a 37 on any of the clay trips or perhaps in West Cornwall on one of the local freights returning to St Blazey during the late afternoon.

This then gives an insight into the main China Clay duties in the region and the purpose of the St Blazey 37s, together with a resume of the lines and traffic that they worked.

There was of course other freight traffic in Cornwall but by 1977 the M5 motorway had opened as far as Exeter and the A38 was a dual carriageway to Plymouth resulting in some loss of freight traffic to road hauliers. Whist in 1978 there was still general freight to Penzance, Ponsandane depot, Truro freight yard, Falmouth Docks, Drump Lane, Redruth, St Austell goods yard, Hayle Wharf and also the sidings at St Erth, it was clearly on the decline.

For many years there were freight services out of St Blazey to destinations 'up country'. These were known by various names such as 'Air Brake Service', 'Speedlink' and 'Enterprise', to name but three. The destinations have varied widely over the years but some of the more regular ones were Severn Tunnel Junction, Temple Mills (East London), Longport, Etruria, Cliffe Vale, Exeter Riverside, Mossend, Carlisle, Gloucester and Newport Alexander Dock Junction.

Forder viaduct, near Saltash, in the evening light, was a wonderful location to catch the Cliffe Vale to St Blazey Enterprise train. Here, 37668 and 37676 provide the motive power on the 9th July 1999 – *Photo R. Geach*

The harbour at Cockwood is a favorite summer evening spot for photography. EWS liveried 37668 and faded two-tone grey 37676, devoid of any sector decals, are pictured on the 1810 St Blazey to Cliffe Vale service passing this location on Thursday 8th July 1999. 37668 was a local engine in the LNLK Cardiff Canton pool while 37676 was in the WKFN sector and based at Toton depot – *Photo R. Geach*

Railfreight Distribution locomotives 37413+37672 working the 6V70 0820 Bescot to St Blazey freight pass the classic location of Horse Cove with the famous Parson and Clerk rocks behind. 26th March 1994 – *Photo S. C. Marshall*

Lea Mount Dawlish gives a superb view in the late afternoon of the 6V70 Bescot to St Blazey passing by with Transrail liveried 37156 and Railfreight grey civil liveried 37262. Both these locomotives had previously spent many years in Scotland. 37156 was by now an Immingham based loco in the FDCI pool and 37262 a Toton locomotive in the ENTN pool. Neither were very common in the far west so this was an interesting pair captured by the photographer. Monday 10th August 1998 – *Photo B. Mills*

The rare sight of a triple-header is seen approaching Exeter St Davids on the 27th July 1991. 37012, in Dutch livery, pilots local engines 37420+37672 on the Bescot to St Blazey service. 37012 was in the DCWA Cardiff Canton Western Civil Engineers pool at this time – *Photo S.C. Marshall*

37521 and 37696 are seen climbing Rattery bank at Dorsley Farm, one mile west of Totnes, with 6C21 1514 Hallen Marsh to Tavistock Junction on Tuesday 27th May 1997 – *Photo S. Crowther*

On a clear Saturday 1st February 1992, 37669 heads up to Dainton summit with the Dover to St Blazey service. The train is formed of Traffic Services branded empty Polybulks, returning from the continent for loading. There was a flow to Basel in Switzerland and also to Sezzadio in Italy via the train ferry. The later service survived longer and ran through the Channel Tunnel – *Photo. B. Mills*

Mainline blue liveried 37065 from the WKBN Toton system wide pool, is seen with the St Blazey to Bodmin Parkway Enterprise trip passing Restormel, just east of Lostwithiel, on the 12th July 1999 – *Photo R. Geach*

In 1989 a considerable new flow was introduced with clay slurry being transported to Irvine in Ayrshire, a return trip of more than 1100 miles. This duty was of course the famous 'Silver Bullet' service, so named because of the bright silver tank wagons used to transport the payload, (though they later became rather tarnished), and was worked throughout by two St Blazey Class 37s in multiple. Despite the huge out and back mileage, very few failures occurred, which is a testament to the expert maintenance at St Blazey and Laira depots

Langford Bridge near Aller Junction on a Sunday morning witnesses the Burngullow to Irvine service behind Railfreight Distribution liveried 37411 and Inter City liveried 37420, both redundant from passenger duties in Scotland and transferred to Plymouth Laira for freight work. 15th September 1991 – *Photo R. Geach*

The 'Silver Bullets' are seen in the snow at Dainton on a cold 15th February 1994 with local engines 37413, in Railfreight Distribution livery, leading 37521, in Railfreight Metals livery. 37521 was a recent transfer into the MDRL Plymouth Laira pool during December 1993 – *Photo S. C. Marshall*

37696, in Railfreight Coal sector livery, along with 37416 in Inter City Livery, make a colourful sight passing Dobwalls with 6S55 Burngullow to Irvine clay slurry service on the 27th October 1994 – *Photo R. Geach*.

The 'Silver Bullets', as they were known, are seen passing through Dawlish, en route from Burngullow to Irvine, running as 6S55 0940 departure worked by local engines 37670+37671 on the 20th July 1990. They conveyed clay slurry for use in the paper industry – *Photo S.C. Marshall*

Let's look at the years from 1980 to 1999 with some selected days to illustrate freight workings around that time: specific issues that affected the Class 37s and changes in motive power are mentioned. Class 37s were not the only motive power used and other types of locomotives are included for illustrative purposes. We will look at the years until 1999 when the introduction of the new class 66 locos had a major impact and severely reduced the use of 37s on the clay workings.

1980

At this time St Blazey still had an allocation of class 25s as well as 37s. Although by the end of autumn the 25s would all be gone. Double-heading of these two types was not unknown and 00:15 hours at Newton Abbot on 12th April produced the sight of 25206 and 37299 heading back to St Blazey with a freight from Exeter Riverside.

On Monday 21st April 1980 25155 worked 7B15 18:35 St Blazey to Friary freight. It was early passing Bodmin Road at 18:07 and right behind was 47145 with 6M26 18:10 St Blazey to Stoke on Trent service. On Tuesday 22nd April 1980 47497 was at work on the Fowey branch with loaded clay for Fowey and a visit at 10:30 hours to St Blazey shed found only one class 37 present, 37299. Alongside were 25155, 25207 and 47246. Later that evening 37299 was observed at Lostwithiel arriving with clay empties from Fowey. This was a poor week for Class 37 observations and only 37299 was seen at work.

The last week of July 1980 brought the astonishing sight of ex-works 37289 on display in Newton Abbot New yard (adjacent the Moretonhampstead branch), the locomotive proudly gleaming in the summer sunshine. Interestingly, on this day, 'Bubble Car' W55025 was used to ferry the public free of charge from Newton Abbot to the yard to visit the freight promotion exhibition, which included several new wagon types as well as MkIII coaches, Prairie tank No.4555, and the 37.

Loadhaul liveried 37516, from the Toton depot WKBN system wide pool, is seen at Lostwithiel yard with the Moorswater cement second portion. The train was brought up the steep climb from Moorswater in two parts because of the weight of the loaded train. 1st August 2000 – *Photo R. Geach*

1981

Any platform enders present at Newton Abbot just after midnight on 11th February 1981 would have witnessed 37206 heading west with the 00:35 Exeter Riverside to St Blazey freight, but rather more surprising was when it worked 4M05 12:50 Penzance to Crewe parcels seen near Menheniot on 17th Feb 1981.

Class 37 visits to Devon were often nocturnal and as such were less recorded and photographed. At Newton Abbot on the 11th March 1981 37274+37142 were observed on a rake of Ferrywagons at 19:30 hours and a daylight sighting on 18th June 1981 at Newton Abbot found Bath Road based 37203 on a special clay service heading west at 16:00 hours. Later that evening 37207+37274 were seen at Teignmouth with the 17:35 St Blazey-Exeter Riverside and on 23rd June 1981 37203 headed a down clay at Newton Abbot at 15:30

There was more double headed action seen at Exeter St Davids at 20:30 hours on the 9th July 1981 with 37299+37207 on the 1735 St Blazey-Riverside & at 21:20 with the 21:15 Riverside-St Blazey return service.

Observations at Dawlish at 20:00 on 3rd August 1981 produced 37142+37203 on the 17:35 St Blazey-Riverside, which returned 90 minutes later. The 17:35 St Blazey to Exeter Riverside regularly produced a class 37 or even a pair. On the 5th August 1981 it was 37206. On the 12th 37206+37299 and on the 17th August 37203 was back again. Then on the 18th it was 37274+37203.

1982

August of this year saw the introduction of the new bogie PBA/JIA Tiger wagons to replace the vacuum braked plank wagons on the Stoke on Trent run. They were also used later on flows to Scotland. A total of 35 were built and could carry a payload of 57.5 tonnes, compared with the old order which conveyed just 13 tonnes.

37206 & 37299 were both active on local workings in Cornwall on Tuesday 24th August, and 47507 worked a loaded train of Cement Presflows to Chacewater. 37142 & 37206 were both seen on St Blazey shed at 14:30 hrs along with 45050 and 47113. 37142 was noted running light through Totnes on the 29th April 1982 towards Newton Abbot, possibly to head down onto the Heathfield branch.

1983

March 1983 found 37158, 37181, 37182, 37207, 37274 and 37281 all busy in Cornwall. Interestingly 37281 was a Canton based loco and 37158 a Bristol Bath Road engine. Type 4s working in the Duchy that month on freight were 45002, 45077, 47056, 47069, 47072 & 47249.

1984

March of the following year found 37176, 37182 and 37207 all busy working local clay traffic. However, March also saw the start of the National Miners strike, which meant that many class 37s throughout the country suddenly became spare. Because of this several strangers appeared in Cornwall such as 37096 and 37307 to name but two, with several more making appearances on passenger duties. The miners' strike was to continue all the way through to March of 1985, just 2 days short of a year in length.

1985

A visit to clay country on 10th April 1985 found 37196, 37207 and 37247 hard at work. 47225 headed the 1741 St Blazey to Severn Tunnel junction Speedlink and 45058 had worked the morning 09:32 St Blazey to Severn Tunnel junction Speedlink, passing Liskeard just after 10am. Unusual Class 37 visitors that year were 37015, 37101, 37120 and 37193.

1986

On the morning of 1st April 1986, 37207 was seen shunting clay wagons at Moorswater. Other class members present in Cornwall that day were 37196 and 37235.

Monday 1st September 1986 found 37235 on the Heathfield duty with 47212+37251 on a 09:30 St Blazey to Severn Tunnel Junction Speedlink passing Liskeard at 10:27. 37135, 37175, 37196 were also in action on clay traffic further west.

On 10th September Cantons' 37304 was observed at work in Cornwall on a train of 20 loaded hoods arriving at Lostwithiel from Rocks at 13:38 hrs. 37175, 37196 & 37207 were the local engines on clay duties that day.

1987

This was the year that the refurbished Class 37s arrived in Cornwall, all looking very smart in their new livery of grey with red stripe and large logo. 37669 to 37675 were delivered in the summer of that year after refurbishment at Crewe works. Changes were also made to the wagon fleet. New CDA wagons were delivered from October 1987 from Doncaster BREL works to replace the wooden hood vacuum brake wagons. The fleet did not enter traffic though until Feb 1988. This was also the year that British Rail reorganised its Railfreight into Sectors.

Another change was the sad closure of the huge Severn Tunnel yard from 12th October. This meant that Speedlink services would run to and from Gloucester.

Wed 22nd April 1987 saw 37175, 37196 and 37207 working Moorswater, Carne Point, Goonbarrow and Parkandillack clay traffic. 50043 was also seen working vice a 37 at Lostwithiel departing at 15:20 to St Blazey with clay empties.

Thursday 3rd September 1987 found refurbished 37672 on the morning Moorswater to Carne Point clay. 37670, 37671 and 37675 were also active in and around Lostwithiel that day.

In 1987 Class 50 No 50049 was the subject of an experiment, being fitted with re-geared Class 37 bogies, renumbered to 50149, and put to work on aggregate traffic in the Westbury area. This was not entirely successful and the experiment was abandoned, with the locomotive heading west to St Blazey, where it spent most of it's time on clay duties. It reverted back to it's original identity in February 1989.

A visit to Lostwithiel on a fine 31st December 1987 found St Blazey short of 37s. No doubt hindered by the loss of 37670 and 37671 which had been badly damaged in an accident at Tavistock Junction Plymouth on the 27th November 1987. 50003 was seen arriving with clay for Fowey at 09:30. It had to wait until 37675 cleared the branch with empties for St Blazey at 09:35. Unusually 08937 was shunting wagons in Lostwithiel yard and then went back light at 15mph to St Blazey just after 10am.

It was busy that morning as 37672 arrived next with clay from Goonbarrow Jn at 10:30 but could not access the branch until 50003 arrived back at 10:42 with its empties which went to St Blazey. 37673 arrived next with two CDAs from St Blazey and attached them to others in the yard before returning light to St Blazey at 11:10. 37675 arrived back at Lostwithiel with another loaded clay set at 11:15 but could not access the branch until another hour had passed as 37672 was still at Fowey. No sooner had 37675 left for Fowey than 50149 arrived with yet another set of loaded CDAs at 12:15. This was a very busy morning at Lostwithiel. My last sighting that day was 37674 on empty CDAs from Carne Point to Tavistock Junction Plymouth passing Liskeard at 16:00 in the last rays of light.

1988

The year started with the wooden OOV Hood wagons still in use. However, the new CDA wagons were brought into traffic in early February and by the 12th had replaced the entire wooden wagon fleet. Class 50149 was still working off St Blazey most of this year vice a 37.

Wednesday 31st August 1988 found 37673, 37674, 37699 & 50149 on clay duties and three days later 37669 was dispatched to Exeter to haul 50004/50031/50007 from Exeter to Laira depot.

Wednesday 9th September 1988 found 50149 at Parkandillack with the Speedlink trip to St Blazey arriving at Par at 15:45. 37672+37673 worked the 15:35 St Blazey to Gloucester Speedlink and unusually 47634 worked a set of CDA empties from Carne Point to Lostwithiel yard at 16:15, returning light to Fowey immediately. It then worked a 16:50 departure of CDA wagons for Rocks.

1989

'Railfreight' became organised into sectors and placed its locomotive fleet into different pools; the Laira China Clay fleet was given the pool code FTLL.

On Sunday 2nd July 1989 37675+37674 passed Liskeard with 6S55 Burngullow to Irvine clay slurry tanks.

During 1989 Laira received its first ETH fitted Class 37/4s which had become redundant in Scotland due to the influx of Sprinter DMUs, particularly on the West Highland line and in the far North. Although these were ETH fitted they were used almost entirely on freight duties.

37412 and 37414 were the first arrivals and on the hot and sunny 6th July 1989 37412 worked a Tavistock Junction to Fowey clay train passing Liskeard at 10:10. Unsurprisingly, the little used Carbis branch closed in August of this year.

1990

During this year the China Clay Pool changed to FCLL Railfreight Distribution based at Plymouth Laira but now came under RFD rather the Trainload Freight.

The first two weeks of July of this year found 37412, 37414, 37669, 37671, 37672, 37673 & 37674 all active and the northbound Irvine (6S55) of 11th July was entrusted to 37671+37414. Normal service was interrupted on Thursday 12th when 37669 failed at Carne Point, halting branch operations for some time that afternoon.

Saturday 14th July 1990 found both 37670 and 37412 on Laira. This may have been the reason for Class 47 No. 47313 joining in with freight operations the following week.

The 6S55 Burngullow to Irvine clay slurry of Wednesday 18th July was in the capable hands of 37671 +37672, and on the same day 47313 was seen at Liskeard with the Heathfield to St Blazey freight. It was then sent out on CDA workings passing Golant at 16:20 for Fowey.

1990 was the year that consideration was given to utilizing 56s on some of the clay workings and a trial was arranged with 56013 on the 27th February to test clearances. The proposal would have seen a reduction in the use of double headed class 37s, with them being replaced by one 56 for services out of the County. However, it was not deemed to be worthwhile and no class 56s were ever used as a result.

1991

1991 was a watershed year for Class 37 activity in Devon. With the rapid run down of the Class 50s and subsequent loss of motive power for use by the Departmental sector, 37s were suddenly making a regular appearance. I well remember standing camera in hand on the platform at Dawlish Warren on a grey Friday 25th January, cursing the weather and lack of action, when grey liveried 37054 and blue 37083 came into view heading a down Departmental working. Not only this, but soon after 37359 went in the opposite direction with the returning oil tanks from Heathfield to Waterston. Suddenly the day was much improved though better was yet to come. I drove back into Exeter just in time to see the 1515 DMU to Barnstaple service depart behind 37146 dragging a deceased 2-car DMU! More of that in another chapter though.

Also, of interest was the flow of coke from Radyr, Abercrombie to Exmouth Junction which normally ran twice a week and brought a Class 37 down to Exeter around lunchtime.

The china clay fleet pool changed again from the 7th July 1991 to MDRL, though the Class 37s were still based at Laira. Another major change during this year was the abolition of 'Speedlink' from July 1991. This inevitably led to the cessation of some of the wagon load clay flows out of the county.

July 1991 saw 37417, 37420, 37670, 37671, 37672, 37673 and 47207 on clay traffic in Cornwall, the first two mentioned taking 6S55 north to Irvine on Wednesday 17th July.

1992

The return slurry tanks from Irvine (6V41) travelled mostly through the night, and thus was less recorded than the northbound train, but on Saturday 15th August 37672+37670 were observed passing through Plymouth North Road station at 08:27 having by this time clocked up more than 1000 miles on their out and back trip. On the same day Exeter St David's stabling point held 37054 and 37254, both Canton engines.

In the same month 37142, 37412, 37413, 37670, 37674 & 37675 were active in Cornwall, 37142 by then a Cardiff Canton loco. On 16th two of these (37413+37675) were sent north with the Irvine.

To add to the variety that month 37521 worked the 12:45 Heathfield-Waterston empty oil tanks on 18th August with 37350 (Ex-D6700) performing on the afternoon Fawley to Tavistock Jn fuel tanks. 37263 arrived at Exeter Riverside from Westbury at 18:45 with a Civil Link service for the Engineers and 37264 arrived on the stabling point at Exeter St Davids.

1993

Monday 5th April 1993 saw 37413 working on the Parkandillack branch hauling 3 Tiger wagons, two Polybulks and a clay slurry tank. Also in action that afternoon was 37674 on empties from Carne Point and Cardiff's 37197 was seen near Par at 17:50. The following day found 37673 at Moorswater and 37670 on the 15:20 St Blazey to Exeter Riverside freight.

Wednesday 7th April 1993 and 37413+37411 passed Rewe north of Exeter with 6S55 Burngullow to Irvine. 37673 worked the 15:20 St Blazey to Exeter Riverside freight passing Starcross just after 6pm and the next day this train had 37670+37197 in charge.

Easter Saturday 10th April found 37098 with 37012 stabled at Exeter St Davids with 47363 and 56073 off the Cardiff Tidal scrap for company.

In December of this year local engines 37411 and 37669 were badly damaged at Burngullow.

1994

1994 saw the launch of the separate freight companies and Transrail became the operator responsible for the clay business. The other companies were Loadhaul, Mainline and Railfreight Distribution. 37695 was rebranded into Transrail livery for the launch of the new business on the 9th September 1994 but the locomotive pools were changed as from the 23rd January, the China Clay pool designated MDRK and based at Cardiff Canton not Plymouth Laira. Thus, Laira no longer had an allocation of class 37 locomotives the first time since 1978.

The pool changed to LNLK from the 20th March 1994 and was now responsible for the running of clay services under the umbrella of Trainload Freight West operation.

During August clay traffic was in the hands of 37229, 37251, 37258, 37412, 37413, 37521 & 37668 with 37037+37141 seen on the retimed 6S55 on Monday 1st August.

37072 37191 and 37521 were present on Exeter stabling point on 5th August with 37142 on a Meldon Quarry to Westbury ballast. 6V62 Fawley to Tavistock Jn fuel tanks that day produced heavyweight 37891.

1995

Class 60 locomotives were now working into Cornwall, which would herald the end of pairs of class 37s on the Burngullow to Irvine. On Tuesday 1st August the new order 60037 was observed working the 16:41 St Blazey to Exeter Riverside freight passing Ivybridge at 18:25.

The last booked Class 37s for the Irvine was on 22nd July, though by this time the train was worked in two stages with a layover at Newport Alexander Dock Jn. Thus the sight of 37670 37669 storming up Dainton with 6B68 0945 Burngullow-Newport on that Saturday lunchtime will live long in the memory.

Also now in the hands of Class 60s was the Waterston to Heathfield oils. However, the year kicked off with 37207+37254 appearing on this train on the 12th January filling in for an unavailable type 5. This pair returned the train to West Wales mid-morning, with 37671+37668 following close behind with the Irvine. A good day to be on the sea wall at Dawlish with a camera!

Also well worth photographing would have been the sight of 37158+47626 on the Penzance to Redhill parcels train on 14th June, the 47 reported as being none too well, hence the assisting loco.

The withdrawal of the final Class 50s and many of the Class 33s offered even more opportunities to see 37s on the one-time LSWR route to Meldon Quarry via Crediton and Okehampton. Various observations during the year revealed 37012, 37035, 37042, 37051, 37162, 37185, 37222, 37263 and 37274. Liveries varied from Dutch to EWS to plain grey and the rather smart Mainline blue. It should be noted that the latter loco quoted in these sightings was the renumbered version of 37308, the number 37274 having been worn by two locomotives. The original D6974 became 37274, then after refurbishment and ETH fitting 37402. All very confusing!

Back in Cornwall 37413, 37521, 37668, 37669, 37670, 37672 & 37696 were seen at work and on 2nd August the unusual combination of 60037+37672 worked the 16:43 St Blazey to Exeter Riverside

1996

This was the year that EWS took over the operation of clay traffic with effect from 21st October 1996. EWS had bought the three Trainload companies and along with RES had taken over the old Trainload business. All the ex BR freight business was now in private hands apart from Railfreight Distribution, but this sector was also eventually acquired by EWS in 1997. Indeed 37668 was repainted in EWS livery for the launch.

Sad news towards the end of the year was the closure of the dries at Moorswater, near Liskeard.

At Par station on Monday 29th July 1996 37230 was on a ballast train working and around lunchtime 37671 was seen at Burngullow loading Polybulks. However the 6V70 0857 Bescot to St Blazey was worked by 60033. Five months later on a wet Tuesday 3rd December 37668, 37671, 37674 and 37696 were all at work on clay trains.

There was still plenty of daytime action on the Okehampton route and booked workings from the quarry included a 7C53 0915 to Exeter Riverside, 6C12 1142 to Westbury, 6O41 1408 to Eastleigh and 7C09 1600 to Westbury in the up direction, with empties arriving on the 7C45 0715 Exeter Riverside to Meldon, 7C08 1000 Westbury to Meldon, 7C13 1200 Westbury to Meldon, and 7C38 1330 Exeter Riverside to Meldon.

Locomotives seen on these duties during 1996 included 37037, 37047, 37079, 37146, 37254, 37274, 37521, 37676, 37715, 37798 and 37803.

1997

On a visit to Lostwithiel on Tuesday 1st April 1997, 37671 was working the morning Tavistock Junction to Carne Point clay service passing Lostwithiel at 10:30 and there appeared to be plenty of clay moving from Marsh Mills (Tavistock Junction) that day. 37521, 37673 and 37674 were all noted that morning with loaded clay trains to Carne Point.

Meldon ballast trains continued to produce the most variety of locomotives and liveries with 37037, 37065, 37072, 37098, 37222, 37242, 37275, 37371, 37513, 37516, 37676, 37694, 37705 & 37798 all noted during the year.

6V62 oil tanks from Fawley to Tavistock Jn was less often a Class 37 now with Class 58s starting to make the occasional appearance. However, 37719 handled the train on 18th August, 37884 on 26th August and 37886 on 5th September.

Also quite regularly producing Class 37s was the Newport (or Hallen Marsh) to St Blazey Enterprise service which was 37674+37521 on 1st September and 37670+37673 exactly a week later.

As expected, the clay slurry from Burngullow to Newport ADJ was regularly the booked class 60. However, on 11th December 37701+37887 made a welcome change.

Good news arrived with new freight flows. The first for transporting heavy rocks from Whatley Quarry to Minehead for use in the new sea defence scheme. This was normally in the hands of a 'heavyweight' Class 37 and 37705, 37707, 37711, 37718, 37798, 37800, 37890 & 37894 were all noted.

The second was an irregular flow of large diameter pipes from Stanton Gate to St Blazey for use by South West Water. This impressive train was not regularly recorded and had first appeared at the end of 1996, with Class 60 60009 in charge, but was seen passing Exeter City Basin on 2nd October 1997 behind the much noisier 37678+37191, and on the 14th October 37670+37674 were seen on the train at Saltash.

Oddities during the year were 37668 with a Swansea to Falmouth Cawoods coal containers on 6th July, 37895+47779 working the RES parcels 1E41 Plymouth-Low Fell passing Teignmouth on 11th August, and 37402 partnering 37219 on 10th September with 7T22 special freight from Exeter Riverside to Swindon. But possibly strangest of all was the pairing of 33046 and 37887 on the 16:13 Exeter Riverside to Tavistock Jn ballast of Thursday 25th September.

1998

By now EWS had overseen operations for over 12 months and many different Class 37s could be seen along with the more regular performers. Things were changing with the introduction of Class 66 locomotives and the older order being phased out, though the invasion into the West Country was still 12 months away.

There was a rare ballast train on the Looe branch on Sunday 3rd May 1998 worked by 37672. Later that day the branch had a visit by 37403 and 37669 with a railtour from Cardiff. On Tuesday 5th May 1998 37713+37895 were noted passing Liskeard at 18:20 with 6M72 17:30 St Blazey to Cliffe Vale service. 37713 in Loadhaul livery, was a rare visitor too. The next day the same pair came back on the Cliffe Vale to St Blazey. 37669 and 37668 were both seen at work in the county that afternoon. On Thursday 7th May 1998 37521, 37672, 37673 & 37713 were all on clay duties around Lostwithiel. Interestingly 37713 wasn't the only Loadhaul liveried loco around that week as 60038 worked the 09:40 Burngullow to Alexander Dock Junction tanks (for Irvine) on the Saturday.

The 37/9 sub-class were never common in the West Country, though the Cardiff to Exeter City Basin scrap train was a possibility. However, the evening of Tuesday 8th December produced not one, but two in the space of a few hours at Exeter St Davids as 6M72 17:00 St Blazey to Cliffe Vale went north with 37178+37906, and 37905 headed west with the 6V62 13:34 Fawley to Tavistock Jn fuel tanks. This was more remarkable as neither of these two had more than a few weeks left in traffic.

6V70 08:57 Cliffe Vale to St Blazey and 6M72 17:00 return were probably the highlight of 1998 being booked for a pair of 37s. Not only that, but the variety of locomotives and liveries was phenomenal. To illustrate this, 6V70 on 5th August was 37057+37680, 10th August was 37156+37262, 18th September 37668+37672 and 5th October 37162+37689. The northbound service 6M72 producing on 6th August 37670+37672 and 8th December 37178+37906.

Fibre cable laying during the year by Eurobell at Paignton required a supply of aggregate from Westbury. This brought the exceptionally rare sight of a freight train onto the Paignton branch. It was an infrequent train at unsociable hours and thus difficult to encounter but 7Z94 05:19 Westbury-Goodrington of 5th September was espied and produced a disappointing, though exceedingly rare, 59101 when seen at Paignton. The locomotive went straight back light engine from Goodrington to Westbury. Eight days later, persistence paid off when 7Z94 0349 Whatley Quarry to Goodrington was headed by 37676+37708, seen nearing Paignton; though anyone sleeping in would have missed it. On Wednesday 28th October 37037+37695 were seen (and heard!) storming up Torre bank with the 15:43 empties back to Westbury, and on 2nd December 37051+37047 produced an almost surreal sight drifting through Torquay station around 8.30am with 7Z94 03:49 Whatley Quarry to Goodrington.

The yard at Exeter Riverside saw plenty of action too in 1998, especially now that a virtual quarry had been created to store aggregate from the Somerset quarries. Delivery was generally in the hands of pairs of 37s pathed as an 03:30 from Merehead and a 15:03 return with 37042+37225 in charge on 19th January, 37057+37255 on 1st April, 37203+37274 on 24th July, 37242+37707 on 30th July, 37013+37509 on 7th August and 37174+37798 on 10th August. The only exception I recorded was 58026 on 30th July of that year.

Oddities during the year were the sight of 37429 in Regional Railways livery climbing Dainton with 7C19 19:40 Tavistock Jn to Exeter Riverside on 5th October, and still around nine days later as it was seen at Exeter with 6C43 13:33 St Blazey to Riverside yard. The same 7C19 was in the charge of 37686 on 8th December, being one of only two left carrying Railfreight Construction decals. The Irvine clay slurry was now worked as two separate trains and the Burngullow to Newport leg was noted behind 37669+37670 on 20th June. Just like the good old days!

1999

The first class 66 to work in Cornwall, 66027, arrived on January 5th with the 14:50 Newport ADJ Enterprise service to St Blazey accompanied by 37683, and the same 66 was seen crew training between St Blazey and Exeter the following day. Both the Newquay and Fowey branches were subsequently passed for class 66 operations.

On Tuesday 16th March 1999 37515+37518 were sent out on 6M72 St Blazey to Cliffe Vale; however, they failed and required assistance from the new order as 66080 went to assist; a reminder to us all that things were going to change very shortly. 66080 was in use at that time on driver training at St Blazey.

There were engineering works at Goonbarrow Jn on Sunday 9th May 1999 and 37671+37515 along with 37698 were seen on various engineers' trains, but the reign of the 37s on clay trains was to diminish quite quickly from the end of June.

66120, 66123 & 66124 all arrived in the UK during mid-June 1999. These three were sent to St Blazey to take over china clay work and all were put into traffic immediately. However, they were not yet cleared on the Parkandillack branch so a 37 had to be retained to work this line. Observations on Monday 12th July found 37668 returning from Fowey to St Blazey with empties arriving at Lostwithiel at 10:38. All other trips on the branch that day were in the hands of the new class 66. However mainline liveried blue 37065 was sent to Bodmin Parkway that evening to collect a couple of vans from Fitzgerald Lighting which were then taken back to St Blazey. 37057+37351 worked the Cliffe Vale to St Blazey Enterprise freight passing Lostwithiel at 19:40. Finally 37676 worked an Exeter Riverside to St Blazey engineer's train passing Lostwithiel at 19:55.

Other Freight Workings

Cement Traffic

The Cement depot at Chacewater was served by rail until 1987 and received cement for distribution from Plymstock. The service was often worked as a block train with type 4 power but class 37s did appear after their arrival in Cornwall.

Moorswater

After the clay works shut it lay dormant for a period before re-opening as a cement distribution point. Until Class 66s were cleared for the route a Class 37 had to be used on this traffic which came from Hope in Derbyshire. Normally worked by a Class 66 to St Blazey. The 37 would be used on the Moorswater branch. The use of class 37s was, however, relatively short lived as Class 66s were eventually cleared to operate on the branch.

An immaculate BR blue 37289 of Landore depot caused something of a stir when it appeared as part of an "Age of the Train" freight promotion exercise at Newton Abbot New Yard. 24th July 1980 – *Photo S. C. Marshall*

37370 (previously 37127), is seen on Moorswater viaduct with the cement empties from Moorswater to St Blazey yard for return to Hope later that evening. 21st March 2000 – *Photo R. Geach*

Coal

Domestic coal was carried for many years in vacuum braked wagons. In 1978, when the 37s arrived, there were rail served coal merchants in Cornwall based at St Austell goods yard and Long Rock, Penzance. In Devon there was a coal concentration depot at Exmouth Junction, Exeter and in Somerset, a coal distribution yard at Yeovil Junction.

37274 takes four wagons of household coal and a brake van into St Blazey yard passing Par signal box on the 16th April 1982. 37274 was a Plymouth loco from October 1980 to April 1983. This coal traffic was soon to cease, with the withdrawal of the vacuum braked wagons – *Photo Transport Treasury*

Freight service operations frequently changed and with the end of wagon load vacuum braked coal wagons the product was conveyed in air-braked Speedlink services. However, with the change to sector management the distribution of coal then changed again. From November 1986 this came under the Speedlink Coal plan. This was renamed Network Coal after the shutdown of Speedlink in July 1991. With the general decline and use of household coal, Network Coal was shut down during 1993.

Former Exeter driver Nick Edwards advises that he learnt Class 37s at Exeter depot and passed out on them in August 1987. The following week he took an evening Speedlink from Exeter to Westbury with 37175 and 31180 in multiple. 37175 was the Exeter training loco at the time and 31180 the loco off the Heathfield trip.

There was a regular service, initially from Abercwmboi (Aberdare) that bought coal from South Wales to the distribution terminal at Exmouth Junction, and also to Yeovil Junction. However the train plans changed often and thus coal came from various yards such as Radyr, East Usk and later from Washwood Heath near Birmingham. These services brought regular Class 37 haulage to Exeter normally running twice a week, but like all freight it changed frequently with extra services run due to demand or cancelled if there was no traffic. As the years passed demand for coal diminished and the services disappeared.

Many different locomotives were seen on the South Wales flow, both refurbished and unrefurbished. It normally ran as 6B37 0525 Abercrombie Exeter and 6C37 1315 Exmouth Junction return.

A brief summary shows the following :-

Jan 1987   37285, 37695
Feb 1987   37199, 37214, 37220, 37230, 37694, 37699
Mar 1987   37158, 37166, 37199, 37217, 37695, 37696
Apr 1987   37167, 37200, 37227, 37230, 37691, 37693, 37694, 37695, 37698
May 1987   37131, 37197, 37426, 37696, 37699
Jun 1987   37250, 37695, 37698
Jul 1987   37690, 37698
Aug 1987   37167, 37212, 37227, 37691
Sept 1987   37196

37285, a long term Cardiff Canton locomotive, is seen passing Exeter Central with the Radyr to Exmouth Junction Network Coal service on Friday 30th January 1987 – *Photo S. C. Marshall*

Cardiff Cantons 37158 is seen descending the bank from Exeter Central to Exeter St David's with the returning 6C37 1315 Exmouth Junction to Abercrombie coal empties on Tuesday 24th March 1987 – *Photo S. C. Marshall*

Transferred from Thornaby depot to Cardiff Canton the previous month, 37200 passes through platform 1 at Exeter St David's with the 6B37 Abercrombie to Exmouth Junction coal service on Tuesday 28th April 1987 – *Photo S. C. Marshall*

37196, by now a Cardiff Canton loco and the former 'Tre Pol Pen', is seen at Exmouth Junction with one empty coal wagon on 9th September 1987. 37196 lost its nameplates earlier that year, with the name being reapplied to the newly refurbished 37671 – *Photo Crowther*

Rural East Devon near Feniton, situated between Honiton and Exeter, and Cardiff Canton based 37227 is seen with just one wagon forming the 6B37 Radyr to Exmouth Junction service on Monday 8th February 1988. With loads like this it is no wonder that Network Coal was shut down – *Photo S. C. Marshall*

One could hardly expect the Burngullow slurry to Newport to produce in 1999 – and yet it did! On Wednesday 31st March 37407 led 37216 with 6B68 0940 Burngullow Jn to Newport.

1999 was the last time that pairs of 37s would be seen with any regularity on the 6V70 / 6M72 'Clayliner' service, and even then a Class 60 could well spoil the best laid plans.

January 29th produced 37264+37698 and February 5th brought 37261+37679. March 1st revealed two stalwarts in 37670+37671 and 25th March produced solo 37698 making a rather loud racket on the climb up to Dainton summit. Friday April 16th found 37671+37698 on the down 6V70 and 37417+37680 on 6M72 that evening. Another trip to Dainton on Monday 19th April produced the spectacular sight of triple headed 37375+37384+37680 with 6V70 which prompted me to venture out the following Monday only to be presented with 47331 on 6V70, which has to be declared as exceedingly rare. 37274 was another solo performer on 28th April with 6V70 and 6M72 of 11th June was 37693 leading 37686. The 18th June found 37672+37198 on the down train and 37896+37887 on the up service, very nice thank you! But the Type 3s were becoming rarer and rarer.

Living near to Dainton was indeed a bonus and previous years had yielded the distant sound of hard working Class 37s, particularly at night when the music carried over the fields, and the pronounced drop in pitch as the train entered the tunnel will live long with me.

My good friend Driver Mark O'Brien of St Blazey depot was also a fan and one evening around 6pm my home phone rang. He was on 6M72 and waiting for the road at Plymouth North Road. "Why don't you mosey on up to Dainton tunnel in half an hour?" he suggested. "These two are a bit special". Clearly I didn't need to ponder too long on that invitation and duly positioned myself with a video camera close to the western portal of the tunnel.

To say that one could hear them accelerating out of Totnes is probably not an exaggeration, and as the noise grew to a crescendo 37057 and 37351 appeared lurching and thrashing around the left-hander on the approach to the tunnel, flickering flames appearing from the exhaust port of the second loco. The locos at that time 37 and 39 years old respectively and the leading one still performing on the main line today, a mere 57 years old!

This wasn't quite the end as the 'Clayliner' did still occasionally produce 37s, and even another triple header on August 3rd with 37678+37377+37153. 37667+37668 were spotted on 6M72 on September 3rd and December 9th found a solo 37042 on 6V70. My only other recorded 37 is that of Loadhaul liveried 37516 slogging – and I use that word deliberately – up Dainton with 6V70 on Monday 10th July 2000.

After that the hills fell silent.

Unusual sightings for 1999 should include green liveried 37350 seen near Totnes in April with 6T92 1250 Tavistock Jn to Westbury and 37216 paired with 37220 on the weedkiller in the same month.

Oil Traffic

For many years there was a service from Waterston to Heathfield that normally ran once a week. The return service was timetabled as 6B20 13:00 Tuesday only Heathfield to Waterston. This service could run early, and a variety of different locomotives were seen over the years. It did produce class 37s, particularly so in the early 1990s, but also class 47s, 56s and class 60s.

Another long-standing freight flow of oil and bitumen ran from Fawley to Plymouth. Many different types of locomotives worked this through the years but from autumn 1991 it was regularly a Class 37, indeed right through the 1990s, until a Class 58 off Eastleigh depot became the norm, and then the Class 66.

There was an Esso oil depot at Hayle Wharfs. Class 37s did visit the branch latterly, but a Class 08 shunter was also used. The visits were spasmodic and short lived with the last train on the branch being in 1981.

Immingham based FDCI loco 37719 passes Dawlish with the 6V62 1334 Fawley to Tavistock Junction fuel tanks on 29th July 1997 – *Photo B. Mills*

Power is clearly being applied to Railfreight Petroleum liveried 37891 as it curves away from Aller Jn, Newton Abbot, and starts the long climb up to Dainton summit with 6V62 Fawley to Tavistock Jn fuel tanks on a beautiful summer's evening of Tuesday 28th June 1994 – *Photo S. Crowther*

Mainline blue liveried 37803 brings 6V62 Fawley to Plymouth petroleum service past Stoneycombe , three miles out of Newton Abbot on Monday 15th July 1996 – *Photo S. Crowther.*

Spruced up after being on display at Aberthaw Power Station open day, EWS red liveried 37411 drifts down from Dainton towards Totnes, passing the quaintly named hamlet of Coombe Fishacre, on 6th May 1997 with 6V62 Fawley to Tavistock Jn – *Photo S. Crowther*

Oil from the West Wales refineries ran to Heathfield oil distribution depot for many years. In this view 37138+37012 are seen at Teigngrace, soon after leaving Heathfield, with the returning empties to Waterston. 18th April 1990 – *Photo S. Woodbridge*

The last service of oil traffic from Waterston, West Wales to Heathfield, near Newton Abbot, ran on Wednesday 17th January 1996, and it is seen at its destination behind Cardiff Canton based 37141. The branch was still used infrequently after this date for clay and timber traffic but has now been mothballed – *Photo S. Crowther*

37669 passes Burngullow with the Tavistock Junction to Penzance Long Rock depot fuel oil on Tuesday 16th March 1999. This traffic originated from Fawley refinery to serve Plymouth along with fuel for Laira depot, St Blazey and Long Rock depots. Sadly no fuel now uses rail transport by rail in the West Country and Fawley no longer dispatches any oil by rail – *Photo R. Geach*

Meldon Quarry Traffic Infrastructure trains and Inspection saloons

A selection of pictures showing the class 37s at work on the Meldon Quarry line and on the various infrastructure services in Devon.

With St Andrews church Colebrook standing high on the hill Dutch liveried 37038 is seen passing Yeoford with an afternoon stone train from Meldon Quarry to Exeter Riverside on 17th September 1991 – *Photo R. Geach*

The 6C12 1142 Meldon to Westbury is seen passing Yeoford on Wednesday 13th November 1996 behind Stewarts Lane based 37375. Interestingly the locomotive is carrying "Mainline" aircraft blue livery without decals – *Photo S. Crowther*

Yeoford on a warm Tuesday 1st August 1995 as 37042 approaches with a short rake of empty ballast wagons for loading at Meldon Quarry. 37042 was allocated to EWCN Toton Trainload freight south GW Infrastructure pool at this time – *Photo R. Geach*

37079 with a Meldon Quarry to Exeter Riverside service passes Cowley Bridge Junction, Exeter on 2nd December 1996. This loco was based at Toton at the time in the Infrastructure North pool ENTN – *Photo R. Geach*

37042+37047 are seen departing Exeter Riverside yard for Westbury, passing Cowley Bridge Junction, with a heavy stone train from Meldon Quarry. 2nd December 1996 – *Photo R. Geach*

Destined to enter preservation locally at the South Devon Railway, 37037 then of Stewarts Lane depot, crosses the junction at Cowley Bridge, Exeter, with a ballast train from Meldon Quarry to Exeter Riverside yard on 17th April 1997 – *Photo S. Crowther*

Coal sector liveried locos from Cardiff Canton, 37704 and 37702, are seen at Exeter St David's stabling point on the 27th December 1993 – *Photo R. Geach*

37174 of Bristol Bath Road depot drops down to Aller Junction at Langford Bridge on 22nd November 1987 with an up ballast train – *Photo S. Crowther*

37521 skirts the Teign Estuary at Bishopsteignton, between Newton Abbot and Teignmouth, with a local ballast working on 15th June 1997 – *Photo S. Crowther*

37197 passes the sight of Cullompton station with the 12:09 Newport to Exeter Riverside ballast working of 14th April 1997. The station was opened in 1844 but closed to passenger traffic in 1964. However, there are tentative plans by the local authorities to reopen it at some point due to the number of new homes in the area – *Photo S. Crowther*

12th April 1997, and the Cardiff Canton pairing of 37263 and 37275 'Oor Wullie' climb towards Whiteball tunnel on the Devon / Somerset border, with an Exeter Riverside to Bristol East ballast working. 37275 was destined to enter preservation locally, firstly at the South Devon Railway, and then from 2018 at the Dartmouth Steam Railway – *Photo S. Crowther*

Seaton Junction, a pale shadow of it's former glory, is seen on 3rd January 1992 as 37263 approaches from the west with an Exeter Riverside to Yeovil Junction engineers train – *Photo S. Crowther*

Just after 4pm on 11th July 1997 and 37707 eases away from Taunton with 8C25 13:15 Merehead Quarry to Minehead, loaded with heavy limestone boulders for use in the Minehead sea defence scheme – *Photo S. Crowther*

As part of the Minehead sea defence scheme, a supply of aggregate and large boulders was required to be transported from the Mendip quarries. This usually ran as an 8C25 13:15 Merehead Quarry to Minehead and is seen being unloaded on 10th April 1997 behind 37711 – *Photo S. Crowther*

37147, recently transferred to Cardiff Canton depot, is seen passing Totnes with Sir William McAlpine's saloon on 29th May 1987 – *Photo S. Crowther*

Just about to enter the western portal of Dainton tunnel on 28th August 1986 is 37430, recently named 'Cwmbran', hauling the private saloon of Sir William McAlpine – *Photo S. Crowther*

Regional Railways liveried 37429 is seen working an Officer's special saloon from Kingswear to Taunton at Aller Junction, Newton Abbot on 3rd July 1998 – *Photo S. Woodbridge*

Mishaps

On the evening of Wednesday 25th November 1987 the 6B43 1545 St Blazey to Exeter Riverside freight was derailed in an accident at Tavistock Junction, 2 miles east of Plymouth. Instead of taking the main line they ploughed on through the headshunt and buffer stops, demolishing a Lowmac wagon that had been parked against them, and digging themselves deep into the earth beyond the stops. The front two freight vehicles in the consist were empty liquefied petroleum gas tanks and, as a precaution, nearby retail premises were evacuated. Thankfully there were no casualties as a result of the accident, but substantial damage was sustained by both locomotives 37670 and 37671, each of which had been released from Crewe Works after full refurbishment just a few months earlier.

Recovery was deferred until the weekend and these two photographs were taken on Saturday 28th November.

In the first view, a steel cable has been attached to the trailing locomotive, 37671, which is being dragged out of the dirt by two class 50s coupled together – *Photo S. Marshall*

The second view shows 37670 still lying where it landed – *Photo S. Marshall*

Weedkiller trains

Many of us looked forward to the first week of April as this was normally the time of the annual visit to Devon and Cornwall by the weedkiller train. The train visited all the branch lines, as well as the main lines but it was the branch line visits that gave us the once a year opportunity to see a loco hauled service on an otherwise all DMU operated railway. In those days the weedkiller was normally fitted into the branch timetable in daylight, thus providing us with some excellent photographic opportunities. Places such as Looe, St Ives, Gunnislake, Falmouth and lesser known locations such as Plymouth Cattewater all received a visit from this train. Normally someone would be able to obtain running times from our friends on the railway. This was essential as the weedkiller could run first thing or later in the evening so advance information was important. Prior to arrival of the 37s the motive power on the Cornish branch lines was a local Class 25. From 1981 no Class 25s were allocated to the far west and thus on the 2nd May 1981, 37232 of Cardiff Canton was seen with the weedkiller train along with 37308 at work on the Gunnislake branch. On 1st May 1982 locally based 37299 was employed on the weedkiller train on the St Ives branch along with class 50018. Rather a rare combination.

For the trip along the Gunnislake branch equally rare 31424 replaced 50018. During the 1984 visit 31293 was the chosen motive power around the Plymouth branch lines. On 6th May 1985 31317 was seen at Exeter with the weedkiller train. I have no records of the weedkiller train in Cornwall that year, but in 1986, locally based 37247 and 37207 were both used; 37247 being observed on the Looe branch on the 27th April.

During April 1987 local based 37196 was used and observed on the Looe branch that year. In 1989 the contracts changed with Hunslet-Barclay providing the traction using top and tail Class 20 locomotives. However this contract was lost to EWS in 1998 so there were once again class 37s on the Cornish Branch Lines. On 10th July 1999 37065 and 37669 were seen on the Fowey branch along with a trip to Parkandillack. Loco haulage did not last long and with the introduction of Railtrack and privatisation, the weedkiller services were then diagrammed to a Network Rail multi-purpose vehicle which brought the end of any exotic 37s to the West Country branch lines on weedkiller trains.

The Looe Valley as seen from on high up the valley near Terras Bridge on an April afternoon in 1987, as the Weedkiller service hauled by 37196 is seen heading for Looe. The river is tidal here and it looks to be just about full tide – *Photo B. Mills*

Bristol bath Road based 37232 leads the Weedkiller train over the magnificent Calstock viaduct on the Gunnislake branch entering Cornwall from Devon. 37308 is on the rear of the train. 2nd May 1981 – Photo B. Mills

On the 29th April 1982, 37299 heads the Weedkiller train on the St Ives branch near Carbis Bay. An interesting formation with 50018 bringing up the rear – *Photo B. Mills*

Chapter 5 – Passenger Duties in the South West

Firstly I should explain that railtours have been deliberately excluded from this section in order to give a more balanced picture. This is not to say that they are irrelevant, far from it, and a separate chapter is dedicated to such trains.

The Change To Diesel-Electric Traction

Dieselisation in the West Country came early, and as we all know, diesel-hydraulics were to be the chosen type of main line diesel traction for the region, as opposed to the diesel-electrics chosen by all others.

Even by the mid-60s only a few diesel-electric types could regularly be seen in the West Country. A pair of BRCW class 33s regularly appeared at Exeter each Saturday with the Brighton to Exeter service, but inter-regional trains would almost always change from diesel-electric traction to a hydraulic at Bristol; to the extent that Bristol was known to us locals as the 'Iron Curtain'. Very occasionally a Brush type 4 (later Class 47) or Class 45 would penetrate the 'Iron Curtain'. One such occasion was when D54 'The Royal Pioneer Corps' appeared on an overnight inter-regional at Paignton on the last day of July 1965. It had come down overnight and headed back north well before 7am, so one had to be up with the lark to glimpse it. Fortunately I was out that morning heading to Exeter and thence to Eastleigh using the 0720 Waterloo service with D803 'Albion', so can vouch first hand for its authenticity.

This was however very much the exception. Generally speaking, hydraulics ruled the roost on both the WR and SR routes to London, the latter retaining steam until 1964 until the Warships diesel-hydraulics took over.

Having said that, the popular long distance Motorail services to the West Country tended to break the mould, and offerings from Stirling, Newcastle and Newton-le-Willows were almost solid diesel-electrics during the mid-60s, again class 45, 46 or 47 being the staple motive power.

Most enthusiasts have a liking for the diesel-hydraulics of the Western Region, and I was no exception, but it's hard to deny that there was something special about the English Electric type 3s and 4s and they certainly found favour with me. Living in Paignton meant that I had to travel many miles to see these EE monsters, and even when Laira received an allocation at the end of the 1970s, they were all outbased at St Blazey for clay duties and therefore made few daytime forays over the border into Devon.

There is an unsubstantiated report of one reaching Laira in or around 1963, possibly connected with the commissioning of the new wheel lathe, though few details have ever come to light regarding this visit and the identity of the locomotive still remains a mystery.

Later, the Cardiff Canton pair of D6881+D6882 worked Paddington to Plymouth and back on 3rd June 1965 as part of a test to ascertain their suitability to such services, and whether a substantial speeding up of the timetable could be achieved. In truth this pair of type 3s performed admirably, though the option was not taken up.

What always seemed strange to me is why they didn't opt for the more powerful pairing of two 'Warship' diesels at that time, a combination that was to be introduced 3 years later. A possible answer may be down to the better riding qualities of the Co-Co type 3s as opposed to the B-B wheel arrangement of a Class 42/43. Increased maintenance of the permanent way may also have been a consideration at the time.

After the high speed tests there was virtually nothing by way of Class 37 action in the peninsula west of Taunton and Yeovil for over a decade. The only known exception was when on 16th April 1969, 6790 fresh off a freight into Exeter Riverside yard, was swiftly dispatched back north on 1M91 Plymouth-Liverpool from Exeter St Davids.

Haulage Opportunities

Summer Saturdays in the South-West were always a time of great anticipation for the rail enthusiast with a flurry of overnight trains heading for Devon or Cornwall.

To illustrate the amazing traffic flow, the list below shows just the southbound overnight passenger carrying services in the summer of 1977.

	Exeter St Davids time
1V37 1933 York-Penzance	02:07
1V39 2135 Nottingham-Newquay	02:41 pass
1V43 2137 Manchester-Newquay	02:56
1V44 2219 Nottingham-Paignton	03:44
1B74 2358 Paddington-Penzance (with sleeping cars)	04:06
1B02 0005 Paddington-Penzance (with sleeping cars)	04:18
1V08 2241 Manchester-Penzance	04:28
1V45 2250 Sheffield-Paignton	04:50
1V52 2040 Newcastle-Newquay	05:31 pass
1V53 2355 Liverpool-Penzance	05:51
1V47 2250 Crewe-St Austell motorail	06:06 pass
1V68 0022 Manchester -Paignton	06:17
1V58 2204 Newcastle- Paignton	06:35
1V55 2340 Hull / 2314 Bradford- Paignton	06:44
1V54 2158 Stirling-Newton Abbot motorail	07:28 pass
1V57 2345 Edinburgh-Plymouth	10:21

All of the long or medium distance services were hauled at the time, with Diesel-Hydraulics, Class 47s and Peaks providing the motive power.

Then, on the bright summer Saturday morning of the 5th June 1976 a locomotive failure at Goodrington carriage sidings was set to change the situation. Stepping forward return diagrams had resolved the situation for a short time but the northbound 1M60 1500 Paignton-Manchester was left without a locomotive and neither Laira nor Newton Abbot, nor the local stabling point at Exeter could produce a spare locomotive. Hence a request was put to Bristol Bath Road for a relief to be sent westwards.

I was fortunate enough to be seated on a bench on the down side at Dawlish station with Roger Griffiths, a local enthusiast, at around lunchtime on that day. We were riding up and down with a variety of motive power and were awaiting 1V69 the 0925 Birmingham-Paignton. I stood up to check whether there was any sign of the aforementioned train approaching. At that exact moment it came into view as it curved past Langstone Rock at the Warren, a good distance away. I squinted my eyes in the heat-haze and stared. "What do you make of that Roger?" I said. "It's a Peak", he replied, getting to his feet. "I'm not so sure", I said. I was unconvinced by his hurried call, especially as my brief glimpse of it on the curve at Dawlish Warren suggested that it was double-headed. Within two minutes it was clear that the Class 37 drought was finally at an end, as 37169 piloting 47089 AMAZON rolled to a halt in Dawlish platform, both locomotives crewed and operational.

Bristol Bath Road depot must also have been hard pressed that morning having little option other than to attach the type 3 to 1V69. 37169, then a Tinsley engine, duly returned north with 1M60, which it took as far as Bristol with the Bristol crew down and back providing traction knowledge. Nowadays, as we all know, 1M60 would have simply been cancelled.

A very early sign of things to come as Tinsley's 37169 stands at Torquay station with the 1M60 1500 Paignton to Manchester service on Saturday 5th June 1976. The 37 had come west as a pilot engine from Bristol to 47089 AMAZON on 1V69 0925 Birmingham-Paignton – *Photo S. C. Marshall*

This was still almost 2 years before Laira would receive an allocation of 37s to replace their ageing Class 25s on clay duties in Cornwall, and by pure coincidence 37169 would, on refurbishment in the late 1980s, become a Laira engine itself, renumbered to 37674. In many ways 5th June 1976 could be described as ground zero.

With all of the Laira allocation of 37s ostensibly based at St Blazey for clay traffic, this meant that any casualty in the Duchy could feasibly fall into the capable hands of a local class 37. Having said that, St Blazey also regularly hosted Peaks, Class 47s and 50s. Most unusual of all was probably the rescue of the down sleepers from Treverrin, near Par, by 56013 – but that's another story.

37267 pilots 50004 on the 1B44 0930 Paddington to Penzance service at Roskear Junction, Cambourne 16th June 1979 – *Photo S. Woodbridge*

Local engine 37142 pilots 50045 on the 1E22 0950 Newquay to Newcastle service into Lostwithiel on Saturday 23rd August 1980. At this time the lovely ex-GWR architecture and signage was still in place on the up side platforms – *Photo C. Moss*

The Class 37 Decades

I had always been a fan of the English Electric Type 3s (later Class 37) and had seen them on my travels from the early 1960s. D6803 arriving at Kings Cross in 1963 with the "Master Cutler" Pullman from Sheffield still stays with me as a wonderful memory, even 50-odd years later.

But the 1970s were generally very bleak regarding any sort of Class 37 activity in the West Country, and it was only very late in the decade, after Laira had received its first small allocation of the type, that any faint hope of finding one in charge of a scheduled passenger train was kindled.

I should mention that for our purposes the geographical area of this article is bounded by Taunton and Yeovil Junction to Penzance including all branch lines of course. I acknowledge that many may argue that Bristol and Salisbury are West Country, but to include further afield locations such as Bristol, Westbury and Weymouth, would make the narrative unwieldy and in some ways defeat the exercise. Weymouth of course, had a booked class 37 turn for many years.

By the late 1970s, with a small fleet of the type now allocated to Laira, I allowed myself to think that the appearance of 37s on passenger duties would become a fairly regular sight. How wrong could I be? I knew that they were outstationed at St Blazey for clay traffic, but regularly saw at least one of them on my frequent visits to Laira depot. This wasn't going to happen. Having said that, I came pretty close on a couple of occasions during 1979.

The first near miss was on Saturday 19th May 1979. This was in an era well before social media information of course. Rob Lewis, a Plymouth based haulage basher and I met at Exeter that morning. Rob and I travelled widely for many years around that time before he suddenly disappeared from the scene.

That morning Rob had managed to acquire a copy of the STN (Special Train Notice) for that day and of immediate interest was a Norwich to Paignton SAGA special due late afternoon and booked for a crew change at Newton Abbot.

In those days boarding such a train was tricky, but far from impossible, and so a plan formulated to be situated at Newton Abbot for around 4pm in order to see if the expected Stratford silver-roofed Class 47 would be on the required list for haulage.

Leaving Exeter at around 3pm we strategically placed ourselves on the western end of the downside platform at Newton Abbot, eagerly awaiting the SAGA special. However the best laid plans, as they say … just before its allotted arrival time we both noticed, almost simultaneously, that the down relief line at Newton Abbot had been pulled off (ie signalled for an approaching train). Nothing else was due as far as we could ascertain and our thoughts instantly focussed in horror on the Norwich to Paignton charter.

But things were about to go from serious to disastrous as a split headcode class 37 loomed into view at the north end of Newton Abbot. Not only that, but our fellow enthusiasts that we had left behind at Exeter, were all waving gleefully to us as the train coasted past behind Stratford's 37064 on the unplatformed relief road. The return working was empty stock and thus we were completely bowled.

My second near miss of 1979 was just two months later.

I lived in Torquay at the time and was in the habit of travelling on 2B33, the 1640 Plymouth-Paignton from Newton Abbot each evening after work. On the evening of Wednesday 25th July 1979 I turned up as usual to take 2B33 for the short run to Paignton, from where a trip to Dawlish on the regular but unadvertised 1815 Paignton-Swindon could be enjoyed, before returning from there with the 1844 Exeter-Paignton stopper. A pleasant evening all round.

25048 duly rolled in on 2B33, then 47262 was taken to Dawlish on the Swindon and 31414 back from Dawlish to Torquay. However my evening run was well and truly ruined when I spoke to an enthusiast on the Swindon train who had seen 37267 working 2B16, the 1000 Paignton-Plymouth earlier that day. Clearly 25048 had been given the kiss of life in order to effect the second part of the diagram. In any event, I took time off work the following morning to view 2B16 at Torquay, but to no avail, as 25048 appeared round the corner from Paignton.

To my knowledge that Wednesday was the only time a 37 worked the train.

In truth 1979 proved to be pretty disastrous from the point of view of my acquiring any class 37 haulage in the West Country. On the evening of Friday 31st August 1979 I travelled north to Yorkshire on the overnight Penzance-Leeds with the aim of 'filling my boots' on the summer-dated holiday trains. Firstly 37209 was bagged on the 0834 Chesterfield-Skegness, then 37057 on the 0925 Sheffield-Blackpool. A swift bus ride from Barnsley to Doncaster found 37069 of Thornaby on the 0835 Newcastle-Yarmouth which was taken to Lincoln, where 37077, also of Thornaby, returned me to Sheffield on the 0940 Yarmouth-Manchester. This was followed by 37115 to Chesterfield, which relieved 45032 at Sheffield on the 1515 Manchester-Harwich, for 37124 of Immingham back to Sheffield with the 1140 Poole-Newcastle.

This was exactly the sort of day I had hoped for and I started to head back west that afternoon as far Derby on the 1639 Leeds-Bristol (47083). Alighting at Derby allowed me to cover a procession of inter-regionals, but this was the point at which I learnt that 37126 of Immingham depot had not only gone west that morning with the 0732 Derby-Paignton, but had actually gone throughout and indeed was due back at Derby quite soon with the 1505 Paignton-Leeds. I was obviously disappointed not to have seen 37126 in my home county but at least would be able to hop aboard for the ride to Chesterfield.

Well that was the theory! In practice the planned crew change at Derby meant that Leeds men worked the train forward, and at that time Leeds Holbeck men didn't know class 37s. Thus to my great annoyance 37126 was hooked off the train before my very eyes, to be replaced by 25318. Quite attractive, I agree, but not part of the plan.

In fact I had a habit of shooting off away from Devon and missing rare class 37 action whilst away. This very nearly happened again in the early hours of Saturday 13th July 1985. This was the day that I started a 7-day all-line railrover, once again accompanied by my good friend Mike Rowe. On such occasions it's always important of course to squeeze every single minute out of the allotted time and we would – let's say – anticipate the starting time of our rover by a few hours, thus heading north from Devon on Friday night's 2035 Plymouth-Newcastle behind 47607.

Now, what always fascinated me was the way Mike was able to sleep at any time of the day or night, even when travelling at speed on a train rocking from side to side. He would slump to a position where his head would vibrate against the window like a woodpecker and yet not raise an eyebrow! Having said this, I do believe I once fell asleep actually standing up on Bristol Temple Meads platform but that's another story....

I mention this only because sleep is an important factor when tackling the stamina-sapping challenge of a 7-day all line railrover without seeing a bed. Now bear in mind that we had only just started our marathon, yet by midnight Mike was heartily knocking away the zzzs.

That's all very well you may say, except that when we rolled to a stop at Birmingham New Street at around 3am I could swear that I heard the 'gurgling' of a class 37. So sure was I that I ventured out onto the platform to hunt down this captivating sound. Jumping down from the open door I soon bumped into a fellow enthusiast who rendered the astounding information that 37082 was stood on the far side of the station with the 2215 Glasgow-Paignton, due out very shortly.

I dashed back to the train, throwing our bags off the luggage rack, and trying without much success to raise Mike. Time was very much of the essence and eventually I managed to heave him off the train and head over the footbridge to the imminent departure for Paignton. We stumbled onto the well filled train with literally seconds to spare and 'enthused' wholeheartedly as the train headed north – yes north! Hang on a minute I thought, but no fear – we soon curved round at Proof House Jn onto the Camp Hill line and thus started our southbound non-stop journey to Bristol Temple Meads.

37082 is seen at Bristol Temple Meads in the early morning light with the previous night's 1V58 2215 Glasgow to Paignton service. 13th July 1985 – *Photo S. C. Marshall*

There was no attempt to remove 37082 from the train at Temple Meads and so a momentous decision had to be made. Do we take 37082 west and then presumably come back with it, or continue our trek north. We somewhat reluctantly decided on the latter with the Summer Saturday 1018 Scarborough to Newcastle being our target, with a quoted 37063, followed by an unquoted Glasgow to Scarborough relief.

In the event 37063 did arrive as planned with the former only to be remarkably replaced by 20068 and 20155 forward to Newcastle. Nevertheless this was taken to Newcastle and then returning to York to head to Glasgow with 37033 on the returning Scarborough relief train.

Into the 80s

This new decade started very much as the 1970s had finished with the occasional Cornish rescue and very little else. One of the few exceptions was on the 13th June 1981 when 37299+37142 worked the 1050 Penzance-Manchester as far as Plymouth.

Saturday 9th July 1983 arrived and followed very much the pattern of 5th June 1976. It was a startlingly beautiful summer's day and I was again at Dawlish, once again with fellow 'haulage basher' Mike Rowe. However, there was a significant difference to the June 76 episode. We had both given up on anything remotely interesting arriving on the long procession of trains from London or the North and, having packed swimming trunks were topping up our tans and taking the odd splash in the sea on the beach just next to Dawlish station. Indeed it was during one of these episodes that I happened to glance once again towards Dawlish Warren. My exact words wouldn't be suitable for publication, but the sight of a 37 approaching whist we were up to our nipples in the English Channel didn't instantly appear to be a good place to be. Even allowing for its station stop we would have no chance to get to the platform in time.

Saturday 13th June 1981 found the 1050 Penzance to Manchester service hauled throughout in Cornwall by local engines 37299 and 37142, seen heading through the former Devonport Junction Plymouth – *Photo B. Mills*

Mike of course couldn't see beyond the end of his nose without his glasses and thus was slightly behind the game as 37076 of Thornaby depot rolled past.

I knew my local timetable and diagrams off by heart and quickly realised that this was an out and back diagram from Saltley, with the 1505 Paignton-Wolverhampton being the back working. However this train was a speedy turnaround at Paignton.

"Quick, quick to the car" I yelled. "No time to change" as we belted up the steps that cross the line at the east end of Dawlish station. My car was parked some way from the beach, so as to avoid parking charges. Still soaking wet and wearing only swimming trunks, I 'wellied' my trusty Triumph Acclaim through the holiday traffic and eventually rolled up at Paignton station with barely 5 minutes to spare. The car was abandoned in the short-stay area outside the station forecourt and Mike and I bailed onto the train without a ticket and still wearing swimming trunks. We bought a ticket on the train and travelled to Exeter St Davids where we alighted. The comments received from friends and passengers alike were quite amusing.

If 1983 was a good year with more Class 37s managing to get beyond what was once the Iron Curtain, 1984 was even better, undoubtedly aided by the miners strike which resulted in spare motive power around the country, and also a good number of relief trains, particularly on the North East to South West axis.

1985 and 1986 continued to produce spasmodic appearances, mostly on summer relief trains from the North-East, but one semi-regular duty appeared whereby a pilot engine was attached to 1C09 0635 Bristol-Plymouth as far as Exeter on Tuesday and Friday mornings. The purpose of this was to position a loco at Exeter for an up freight from Riverside yard to Bristol East, though naturally no freight traffic meant no pilot engine, meaning that there was no guarantee that the train would be of particular interest.

Still living in Torquay meant that this train was extremely difficult to reach, and in most cases any working was known only after the event. However, on Tuesday 11th February 1986 I crawled out of bed at some unearthly hour and made a telephone call to a railway friend to ascertain whether any gen was known regarding 1C09 that morning.

Should a move be required, the 0600 Plymouth-Paddington HST included a very handy Tiverton Junction stop giving a small plus connection into 1C09 heading in the opposite direction.

"Looks like you might be in luck", was the reply, "37078 is planned to pilot the train to Exeter". No sooner had I replaced the handset than I was dressed and speeding towards Newton Abbot in the car. Confirming that the 0600 Plymouth-Paddington was on time, "Day return Tiverton Junction please" and I was on my way.

This was a particularly awkward train to cover and thus I only attempted it on 6 occasions, usually without any advance knowledge of the loco allocation.

28th Dec 1984 produced 50015 with no pilot loco
21st May 1985 produced 45069+50012
11th February 1986 produced 37078+50012
14th February 1986 produced 37232+47431
11th April 1986 produced 47616 with no pilot loco
29th April 1986 produced 50001 with no pilot loco

A full list of known pilot workings on 1C09 are shown in Chapter 9.

On Saturday 9 July 1983, 37076 of Thornaby depot is seen passing Dawlish Warren with 1V73 0820 Liverpool to Paignton service – *Photo S. C. Marshall Collection*

37233 waits time at Torquay with the 1715 Paignton to Birmingham New Street relief on 28th August 1984. Of all the hundreds of passenger duties performed by the class in the West Country by far the vast majority were last minute rescues or substitutions. However this particular train was an exception and was known to be booked for a Class 37 more than two weeks in advance – *Photo S. C. Marshall*

Saturday 18th May 1985 brought an interesting visitor to the South-West when 37197 powered the 1V71 0820 Liverpool to Paignton train forward from Birmingham New Street, seen here taking the Paignton route at Aller Junction, near Newton Abbot – *Photo S. Crowther*

37024 was a Tinsley locomotive when it was tasked to work throughout with the 1V32 1030 York-Penzance relief on Saturday 27th July 1985, seen here at Plymouth – *Photo S. Woodbridge*

Exeter St Davids on Tuesday 11th February 1986 and Thornaby based 37078 'Teesside Steelmaster' made a rare appearance when it piloted 50012 'Benbow' on 1C09 0635 Bristol-Plymouth as far as Exeter. It returned north later that morning with a freight from Riverside yard – *Photo S. C. Marshall*

A very rare event is captured on film just before 8pm on Friday 27th July 1984 as Laira's 37181 arrives at Newton Abbot with a 19:23 Paignton to Glasgow Central overnight service which 37181 worked to Bristol – *Photo S. Crowther*

Power Car Problems

Heading westwards beyond Newton Abbot the railway terrain changes dramatically. The Somerset levels are left far behind, where only Whiteball, on the Devon & Somerset border would provide any hill climbing difficulties. However, almost immediately on leaving Newton Abbot westwards, one would encounter the steep climb to Dainton tunnel, followed swiftly by Rattery, which is particularly difficult when attempted from a standing start out of Totnes. In an easterly direction, Rattery is no problem, but the fierce climb up Hemerdon starts soon after passing Tavistock Jn, and then of course Dainton has to be surmounted as that is a fierce climb in both directions.

Inter-City 125s (High Speed Trains) were causing more problems than most traction types at that time, particularly through loss of coolant and subsequent overheating. Their high gearing meant that the loss of one power car, for whatever reason, would result in a difficult task for the remaining powering unit on the hills west of Newton Abbot. Because of this, a decree was brought in that HSTs on only one power car should be piloted over the Devon banks.

In the early period this was often a Class 47 or a Class 50, or sometimes a Class 45/46 Peak locomotive, but occasionally more exotic motive power was used, such as Class 31, Class 33, Class 56 and even on one occasion a Class 58, though this had come on at Birmingham New Street, not Exeter or Plymouth, which was the more commonplace for attachment. Also in this case both power cars had been shut down.

However, by the end of the 1980s class 37s were becoming far more regular in Devon and with Exeter drivers now trained on them the scope was much enhanced.

It should be stressed at this point that not only HSTs struggled with the Devon banks. Many types have proved unable over the years to meet the challenge. The Virgin Cross Country Class 47s, particularly in their latter years, often required assistance and more than the odd 50 has got into trouble as well.

37299+37274 depart Plymouth station with 1A13 1045 Penzance to Paddington service on Saturday 4th September 1982 which they worked as far as Exeter St Davids that day – *Photo B. Mills*

37207 has arrived at Plymouth Station with the delayed 0918 Edinburgh to Plymouth service on Saturday 7th August 1982 – *Photo B. Mills*

Wet weather affects rail adhesion of course and this had to be taken into the equation when deciding if a train was fit enough to tackle the banks. The pinnacle of 'entertainment' was on Sunday 7th July 1991, when no less than 5 HST drags occurred on one day. Three different Class 37s and a Class 50 were used during that day to assist.

Based on the above, I don't want the reader to be left with the idea that the whole of the Cornish main line is like a billiard table. Far from it. The inclines may not be quite as fierce as Dainton, Rattery and Hemerdon, but there are stiff climbs out of Bodmin Parkway to Doublebois, Lostwithiel (westwards) and Par (eastwards), to mention but three. To add to the problems west of Plymouth, much of the route comprises of a series of sweeping reverse curves and rain can be frequent and heavy in this far-flung part of the country, combining with lush lineside foliage to produce a lethal reduction in track adhesion.

The 1990s

With more Exeter drivers being trained on Class 37s in 1991, coupled with the replacement of DCWA engineer Class 50s with Canton 37s at Exeter, the scope for Class 37 haulage in the West was markedly increased and 1991 proved to be the watershed year.

On the cold and grey afternoon of 23rd January 1991 I was heading back from West Devon to my base in Exeter and encountered a queue of traffic at the closed level crossing gates at Red Cow crossing at the north end of St Davids station. The radio in my car was blaring away and thus I hadn't heard the departure from St Davids station that was about to materialise. There in all it's glory was 37146, now of Canton depot, late of Motherwell, drifting past hauling a first generation DMU set. Not only that, but in the fading light I could clearly see passengers aboard the DMU.

Saturday 21st July 1990, and 37669 heads under Shaldon Bridge, on the approach to Teignmouth, with the 1S04 10:00 Penzance to Edinburgh HST service, which it assisted from Par to Bristol Temple Meads – *Photo S. Crowther*

37083 after arrival at Plymouth with the 1C54 1635 Paddington to Plymouth on 11th March 1991. It had piloted the train from Exeter – *Photo S. C. Marshall*

Plymouth station on the 27th May 1991, and 37035 has arrived with the 1C32 1135 Paddington to Plymouth. This loco also topped the 1C66 1835 Paddington to Plymouth service that day from Exeter St Davids – *Photo S. O'Dell*

Previously based on the Eastern Region for many years 37098, by now allocated to the Civil Engineers sector at Cardiff Canton, coasts to a halt at Teignmouth station on Saturday 24th August 1991 with 1M86 1345 Paignton-Nottingham. The HST had encountered difficulties on the down train earlier in the day, and both power cars, 43042 & 43088, had at this point been shut down. Interestingly, 37098 came to the assistance of no less than three trains on this particular day – *Photo S. C. Marshall*

A fine evening at Paignton as 37158 leads 37092 and 37197 with an additional return service from Paignton to Paddington, run in conjunction with a diesel gala on the (as was) Paignton & Dartmouth Railway 20th June 93 – *Photo P. Gardner*

Passengers look on with interest as 37207 coasts into Paignton station from Goodrington yard complete with a West Coast Mk III set and driving van trailer to form the 1705 Paignton-Manchester on Saturday 27th July 1991. The 37 would work as far as Bristol Temple Meads, replaced there by a class 47 – *Photo S. C. Marshall*

On Saturday 10th August 1991 the 1030 Paddington-Penzance HST was declared a failure near Lavington in Wiltshire. 37254 was commandeered to assist the train forward and is seen climbing Dainton bank, close to Stoneycombe Quarry. The 37 took the train all the way through to Penzance – *Photo S. Crowther*

37141 climbs Rattery bank, west of Totnes, with the 1335 Paddington-Penzance service of 7th September 1996 – *Photo S. C. Marshall*

Retro repainted into BR green, pioneer of the Class 37350 (ex-D6700), arrived at Paignton in the wee hours of Saturday 12th June 1999 with the previous nights 2330 from Manchester Piccadilly. It stayed in diagram, returning with the 1S66 0855 Paignton-Glasgow and is seen here at Newton Abbot on its way back north as far as Bristol – *Photo S. Woodbridge*

In an instant I realised that it had to be a Barnstaple service and within seconds had spun the car around to be heading back in the direction I had come, but this time following Crediton signs.

To beat the ensemble to Crediton was far easier than I had envisaged and thus I was able to take the train to Barnstaple and back, finding several local enthusiasts already aboard. This was before the general availability of mobile phones of course. Hence the sparsity of information about this working, though local sources now suggest that it may possibly have occurred also on the previous day.

Soon after this event a local telephone network was put into place with almost military precision so that word could be spread down the line if a sighting had been noted by any of our group.

Many of the branch lines in Devon and Cornwall also saw Class 37s on passenger duties over the years. We have already mentioned the Paignton and Barnstaple routes but the Exmouth, Newquay and Falmouth branches also witnessed a 37 hauled service train at least once. Railtours also operated to Okehampton, Heathfield, Kingswear, Buckfastleigh, Bere Alston, Bodmin General / Boscarne Jn, Fowey, Looe, Parkandillack and St Ives.

However, one route that we haven't mentioned so far is the ex-LSWR route from Exeter to London Waterloo. 37s featured quite prominently on this line primarily because of the poor availability of the Class 47s and Class 50s in use on these services.

Reliability of the first generation DMUs around Exeter was at an all-time low during 1990 and 1991. 1990 had seen the amazing sight of Class 33s, Class 50s and even the odd Class 47s used on an emergency 3 coach Mk1 set, or even hauling a dead DMU, on branch line services to Barnstaple. However, with the civil engineers Class 50s being withdrawn, their replacements, the Class 37s, were now available to step into the breach and previously unimagined sights such as this were becoming more commonplace. 37141 stands at Exeter Central having run round the empty stock to form the timetabled 2B80 1730 to Barnstaple on 3rd April 1991 – *Photo S. Woodbridge*

Just over a month after the previous photograph was taken, 37010 stands at Barnstaple, having arrived with 2B78 1605 from Exeter Central. Friday 24th May 1991 – *Photo S. O'Dell*

37207 is seen at Bugle station hauling a failed DMU on a Par to Newquay service on Sunday 17th July 1983. The 37 was used on numerous services that weekend due to the failure of the branches diesel unit set – *Photo B. Mills*

On 21st June 1992 a relief train was operated by BR from London Paddington to Paignton in connection with the diesel gala on the Paignton & Dartmouth Railway. This was powered by a Class 56 between Paddington and Exeter, but the Exeter to Paignton legs were worked by 37672. This is the view at Torquay of the 1Z22 0800 Paddington-Paignton – *Photo S. Crowther*

Saturday 13th June 1998 produced possibly the working of the decade in the West Country as the summer Saturday only 0814 Edinburgh to Newquay HST arrived at Exeter in need of assistance. Large logo liveried 37025 'Inverness TMD' was duly commandeered from the stabling point to take the train forward. Amazingly the train went all the way through to Newquay, despite there no longer being any run-round facility at this destination. The rear power car, which of course became the front car for the return, was coaxed into life to lead the train back to Plymouth with 37025 idling at the rear – *Photo S. O'Dell*

Although the type 3s appeared very occasionally on the London end of the line east of Salisbury, it is further west that our interest lies. Early 1989 found the first recorded use on this route when 37239 was beckoned from Exeter to Axminster to rescue the 1100 Waterloo-Exeter. Then in November 1990 37191 hauled a 1Z40 1505 Exeter to Salisbury additional, following the failure of the booked service. And on Christmas Eve 1990 37158 performed between Exeter St Davids and Honiton instead of a failed first generation DMU on a local commuter train.

Class 47s were the staple power on the ex-LSWR route from Exeter to Waterloo in 1992 following the demise of the Class 50s, but availability was poor, and Class 37 could be seen quite frequently as last minute replacements. This was the case at Yeovil Junction on Thursday 16th April 1992 where 37010 is seen at the head of the 1738 Exeter-Waterloo service. It was removed from the train at this point and swapped over onto the incoming 1655 Waterloo-Exeter, thus returning the 37 to Exeter for it's Civil Engineers duties – *Photo S. C. Marshall*

Another day – another rescue, as 37230 rolls into Axminster towing 47579 on 1V10, the 1047 Basingstoke-Paignton, on Saturday 13th June 1992 – *Photo S. C. Marshall*

By 1991 emergency use of Class 37s on this route was becoming more regular as the booked motive power struggled with availability. Trips along the whole route from Exeter to Waterloo by 37s were rare and only happened on a very few occasions, but Friday 23rd August 1991 became a red letter day when 37258 worked throughout from Plymouth to Waterloo and back to Exeter, which eclipsed all others on this route.

By chance I had taken a day off work that Friday and popped down to St Davids station to have a quick scan of the motive power on the stabling point. My interest level shot up when a member of staff (also an enthusiast) approached me to mention that 37258 had just shot off light engine to Plymouth and the rumour was that the loco for 1O40 1355 (FO) Plymouth-Portsmouth Harbour had failed.

As often was the case, I had a local runabout ticket in my pocket and validity was no problem, so I headed down to Plymouth on the first available service to be greeted by the sight of departmental grey liveried 37258 stood on a rake of NSE Mark II stock. Not only that, my good friend, Driver Nick Edwards was at the controls.

This provided an exhilarating run over Hemerdon and Dainton and along the sea wall, but interestingly the train never did reach Portsmouth Harbour. This was because the locomotive for the 1428 Exeter-Waterloo had been declared a failure at Exeter and thus the 1355 train from Plymouth was diverted to Waterloo to run in its place, albeit late. With no replacement available at Salisbury, 37258 duly ran all the way through to Waterloo, returning in diagram on 2V21 the 1915 to Exeter St Davids.

For the rest of that decade passenger workings became quite common, as will be seen by the tables listed at the end of this chapter. Only two were noted after the end of the decade, one in 2002 and one in 2004 but it was fun while it lasted.

Still wearing Coal Sector decals, 37213 stands at Paignton on Saturday 25th June 1994 having just arrived with the 0605 train from Glasgow Central. The 37 took over the train at Exeter and worked back as far as Bristol with the returning 1603 Paignton-Liverpool – *Photo S. O'Dell*

On its last ever passenger duty, a shabby looking 37225 of Immingham depot, waits to be removed from the 1140 Plymouth-Liverpool at Exeter St David's on Tuesday 16th December 1997. The train loco 47839 had been declared low on power on the way down and was not allowed over the Devon banks unassisted – *Photo S. O'Dell*

Penzance station on the morning of Saturday 15th August 1998 and two refurbished members of the class, 37897+37679, await departure with 1M56, the 0840 to Manchester Piccadilly. They had arrived the previous evening with the 0840 from Glasgow Central – *Photo S. O'Dell*

A striking view at Exeter St David's on the evening of 9th June 1998 as 37025 'Inverness TMD' waits for the road west, having been attached to the 1502 Newcastle-Plymouth HST – *Photo S. O'Dell*

CLASS 37 PASSENGER WORKINGS IN THE WESTERN PENINSULAR

(South of Taunton and West of Yeovil Jn)

The data that follows, been compiled and researched over many years. Every effort has been made to ensure that the information is correct. However, such an enormous task is fraught with danger, and in the days before social media, many details were passed on only by word of mouth. As such, occasional errors and conflicts may arise.

Some reports have been omitted because they are unverified and too preposterous to include, but others that have been solely reported in contemporary printed material such as railway periodicals are included but signified by the symbol † in the third column.

Railtours (see chapter 7) are generally excluded from the list. However we acknowledge that there are services that may overlap the boundary between a railtour, a charter, a relief train and other specials, so an objective view has been taken.

Chapter 8 at the rear of the book illustrates the same data but sorted by sequence of the locomotive number.

Should anyone be able to add or correct any of this information by way of a definite sighting then we would be pleased to receive any details at the email address 37westinfo@gmail.com so that we can update our database.

TABLE A

Log	Loco	†	dy	date			from	to	code	train	notes
1	D6881+D6882		Th	3	6	1965	Paddington	Plymouth		....PadPly	passenger trials
2	D6881+D6882		Th	3	6	1965	Plymouth	Paddington		....PlyPad	passenger trials
3	6730		We	16	4	1969	Exeter	Bristol	1M91	0740PlyLvↄ	pilot to D1054
4	37169		Sa	5	6	1976	Bristol	Paignton	1V69	0925BnsPgn	+47089(T)
5	37169		Sa	5	6	1976	Paignton	Bristol	1M60	1500PgnMↄp	
6	37142	†	Fr	8	9	1978	St Germans	Penzance	1B02	0005PadPnz	+25080(T)+47445(DIT)
7	37064		Sa	19	5	1979	Norwich	Paignton	1Z..	0910NrwFgn	Saga relief
8	37050		Sa	26	5	1979	York	Newton Abbot	1V81	1043YrkNab	motorail
9	37050		Sa	26	5	1979	Newton Abbot	York	1E00	2230NabYrk	motorail
10	37267		Sa	16	6	1979	Par?	Penzance	1B44	0930Padↄnz	+50004
11	37142		Sa	16	6	1979	Par	Newquay		1200ParNqy	with a class 47
12	37142		Sa	16	6	1979	Newquay	Par	1M31	1402NqyBns	with a class 47
13	37267		We	25	7	1979	Paignton	Plymouth	2B16	1000PgnPly	
14	37267		Tu	14	8	1979	Totnes	Exeter	1M74	1356PnzBns	+46026(DIT)
15	37126		Sa	1	9	1979	Derby	Paignton	1V62	0732DbyPgn	
16	37126		Sa	1	9	1979	Paignton	Derby	1E91	1505PgↄLds	25318 forward
17	37183		Tu	15	1	1980	Cardiff	Plymouth	1B26	0756CdfPly	
18	37183		Tu	15	1	1980	Plymouth	Cardiff	1C60	1330PlySwa	
19	37142		Fr	27	6	1980	Bodmin Road	Plymouth		0620PnzPly	47027 loss of power
20	37299		Fr	8	8	1980	Par	Plymouth	1E61	1808PↄzLds	+45031
21	37142		Sa	23	8	1980	Newquay	Plymouth	1E22	0950NqyNcl	+50045[DIT]
22	37233	†	We	8	10	1980	Par ?	Penzance	1V76	0920LvpPnz	
23	37207	†	Su	11	10	1980	Plymouth	Lostwithiel	2B12	1000PlyPnz	+47482(DIT)
24	37299		Tu	25	11	1980	Par	Exeter	1A59	1332PnzPad	+HST
25	37208		Th	9	4	1981	Plymouth	Exeter	1A79	1008PↄzPad	+HST
26	37203		Sa	9	5	1981	Plymouth	Penzance	2B36	1745PlyPnz	
27	37203		Sa	16	5	1981	Plymouth	Penzance	2B36	1745PlyPnz	
28	37203		Fr	22	5	1981	Par	Plymouth	1E21	1025PnzLds	+50016(T)
29	37203		Sa	23	5	1981	Plymouth	Penzance	2B36	1745PlyPnz	
30	37142		Sa	30	5	1981	Plymouth	Penzance	2B36	1745PlyPnz	2 coaches
31	37299+37142		Sa	13	6	1981	Penzance	Plymouth	1M83	1050PnzMcp	

Log	Loco	†	dy		date		from	to	code	train	notes
32	37142		Sa	1	8	1981	Par	Plymouth	1A09	1035 NqyPad	+47324
33	37274+37206		Su	22	11	1981	Par?	Plymouth	1A07	2135PnzPad	
34	37208		Sa	30	1	1982	Plymouth ?	Exeter	1A59	0900PnzPad	+HST
35	37102		Mo	7	6	1982	Torquay	Birmingham	1E12	1115 TqyNcl	Saga train
36	37207		Sa	7	8	1982	?	Plymouth		0918 EdbPly	+HST. 112 late at Plymouth
37	37206		We	11	8	1982	Plymouth	Lostwithiel	2B87	1620PlyNqy	
38	37207		We	11	8	1982	Lostwithiel	Newquay	2B87	1620PlyNqy	+(37206)DIT
39	37274		Sa	14	8	1982	Par	Newquay		....ParNqy	+DMU
40	37274		Sa	14	8	1982	Newquay	Par		....NqyPar	+DMU
41	37274+37299		Sa	4	9	1982	Plymouth	Exeter	1A13	1045PnzPad	+37299(M)+HST
42	37274		Su	12	12	1982	Par?	Exeter	1A07	2135PnzPad	+50048(T)
43	37207+37182	†	Su	30	1	1983	Exeter	Plymouth		1230EdbPly	+HST
44	37181	†	Sa	28	5	1983	Tremake	Penzance	1Z50	1147PadPnz	+47581(DIT)
45	37076		Sa	9	7	1983	Birmingham?	Paignton	1V73	0820LvpPgn	
46	37076		Sa	9	7	1983	Paignton	Wolverhampton	1M54	1505PgnWpt	
47	37270		Su	10	7	1983	Par	Newquay	2B87	1715ParNqy	+DMU
48	37270		Su	10	7	1983	Newquay	Par	2B87	1858NqyPar	+DMU
49	37207		Sa	16	7	1983	Par	Newquay	2B87	0712ParNqy	+DMU
50	37207		Sa	16	7	1983	Newquay	Par	2B87	0810NqyPar	+DMU
51	37207		Sa	16	7	1983	Par	Newquay	2B87	1305ParNqy	+DMU
52	37207		Sa	16	7	1983	Newquay	Par	2B87	1405NqyPar	+DMU
53	37207		Sa	16	7	1983	Par	Newquay	2B87	1645ParNqy	+DMU
54	37207		Sa	16	7	1983	Newquay	Par	2B87	1740NqyPar	+DMU
55	37207		Sa	16	7	1983	Par	Newquay	2B87	1955ParNqy	+DMU
56	37207		Sa	16	7	1983	Newquay	Par	2B87	2110NqyPar	+DMU
57	37270		Sa	16	7	1983	Truro	Plymouth	1B61	1815PnzBtm	+47334(T)
58	37207		Su	17	7	1983	Par	Newquay	2B87	1205ParNqy	+DMU
59	37207		Su	17	7	1983	Newquay	Par	2B87	1340NqyPar	+DMU
60	37207		Su	17	7	1983	Par	Newquay	2B87	1510ParNqy	+DMU
61	37207		Su	17	7	1983	Newquay	Par	2B87	1610NqyPar	+DMU
62	37207		Su	17	7	1983	Par	Newquay	2B87	1715ParNqy	+DMU
63	37207		Su	17	7	1983	Newquay	Par	2B87	1858NqyPar	+DMU

Log	Loco	†	dy		date		from	to	code	train	notes
64	37207-37181		Mo	29	8	1983	Lostwithiel	Penzance	1V76	0920LvpPrz	+37181(M)+50049(DIT)
65	37272		Su	25	9	1983	Par?	Exeter	1A07	2135PnzPad	+50038[T]
66	37207		Tu	5	2	1984	Par	Plymouth	1A02	2135PnzPad	+50030(T)
67	37269		Mo	9	4	1984	Plymouth	Bristol	1M85	0740PnzLvp	+50028(T)
68	37 81		Su	15	4	1984	Par	Plymouth	1A07	2135PnzPad	+50029(T)
69	37207	†	Tu	14	5	1984	Par	Penzance		?	+47553(DIT)
70	37075		Sa	2	6	1984	Newcastle	Plymouth	1V48	2030NclNqy	
71	37181-37307		Sa	9	6	1984	Penzance	Plymouth	1Z26	0545PnzWem	Hockey special
72	37275		Sa	23	6	1984	Birmingham	Paignton	1V71	0820LvpPgn	
73	37275		Sa	23	6	1984	Paignton	Birmingham	1M65	1608PgnLvp	
74	37273		Sa	7	7	1984	Penzance	Plymouth	1M44	1125pnzmcp	50031 from Plymouth
75	37207		Su	22	7	1984	Par	Newquay		1510ParNqy	+DMU
76	37207		Su	22	7	1984	Newquay	Par		1650NqyPar	+DMU
77	37207		Su	22	7	1984	Par	Newquay		1815ParNqy	+DMU
78	37207		Su	22	7	1984	Newquay	Par		1950NqyPar	+DMU
79	37299		Fr	27	7	1984	Bristol	Silk Mill		1030YrkPly	rescued by 31317
80	37131		Fr	27	7	1984	Paignton	Bristol	1S81	1928PgnGgc	
81	37251		Tu	31	7	1984	York	Plymouth	1V31	1030YrkPly	
82	37307		We	1	8	1984	Par	Newquay		1138ParNqy	+DMU
83	37307		We	1	8	1984	Newquay	Par	2C83	1325NqyFar	+DMU
84	37273		We	1	8	1984	Newquay	Plymouth		0950NqyPly	
85	37096		Th	9	8	1984	York	Plymouth	1V31	1030YrkFly	
86	37031		Fr	10	8	1984	York	Plymouth	1Z49	1420YrkFly	
87	37207+37247		Sa	11	8	1984	St Germans	Liskeard	1V64	0717DbyFnz	on rear of train 4743 failed
88	37096		Sa	11	8	1984	Liskeard	Penzance	1V64	0717DbyFnz	+47143(DIT)
89	37307		Mo	20	8	1984	Par	Penzance	1Z18	0922LdsPnz	+45120(DIT)
90	37275		Fr	24	8	1984	Bristol	Plymouth	1V49	1420YrkPly	
91	37207+37181		Sa	25	8	1984	Plymouth	Exeter	1A79	1448PnzPad	+37181(M)+HST
92	37266		Sa	25	8	1984	Sheffield	Paignton	1V49	1521SfdPgn	
93	37233		Tu	28	8	1984	Paignton	Birmingham	1Z18	1715PgnBns	
94	37185		Sa	8	9	1984	Par	Penzance		0917ParPnz	scratch relief
95	37177+37219		Sa	22	9	1984	Birmingham	Paignton	1V71	0820LvpPgn	+37219(M)

Log	Loco	†	dy	date			from	to	code	train	notes
96	37219+37177		Sa	22	9	1984	Paignton	Birmingham	1M65	1608PgnLvp	+37177(M)
97	37281		Sa	10	11	1984	Par	Penzance	2C68	0545BplPnz	+50020(DIT)
98	37281		Su	11	11	1984	Par	Plymouth	1A02	2135PnzPad	+47624(T)
99	37099		Fr	25	1	1985	Bristol	Exeter	1C09	0635BtmPly	+50009(T)
100	37267		Fr	1	3	1985	Bristol	Exeter	1C09	0635BtmPly	+50020(T)
101	37181	†	Fr	12	4	1985	Bodmin Parkway	Lostwithiel	1V76	0936LvpPnz	propelling 45131
102	37196	†	Fr	12	4	1985	Lostwithiel	Penzance	1V76	0936LvpPnz	+45131(DIT)
103	37182		Fr	17	5	1985	Bristol	Exeter	1C09	0635BtmPly	+47492(T)
104	37197		Sa	18	5	1985	Birmingham	Paignton	1V71	0820LvpPgn	
105	37052		Sa	22	6	1985	Birmingham	Paignton	1V58	2215GgcPgn	
106	37052		Sa	22	6	1985	Paignton	Birmingham	1M86	1000PgnLvp	
107	37246		Fr	5	7	1985	York	Plymouth		1425YrkPly	
108	37082		Sa	13	7	1985	Birmingham	Paignton	1V58	2215GgcPgn	
109	37082		Sa	13	7	1985	Paignton	Birmingham	1M86	1000PgnLvp	
110	37082	†	Mo	15	7	1985	Birmingham	Newton Abbot		1020GgcPly	failed-train terminated
111	37024		Sa	27	7	1985	York	Penzance	1V32	1030YrkPnz	
112	37024		Su	28	7	1985	Exeter	York	1E92	1340ExdYrk	
113	37196		Tu	30	7	1985	Par	Plymouth	1A73	1346PnzPad	+HST
114	37101		Su	11	8	1985	Derby	Plymouth	1V40	1055DbyPly	
115	37207		Sa	17	8	1985	Menheniot	Penzance	1C21	0805SwaPnz	+47246(DIT)
116	37058		Sa	17	8	1985	York	Penzance	1V32	1030YrkPnz	
117	37061		Mo	19	8	1985	York	Penzance	1V32	1030YrkPnz	
118	37165		Sa	24	8	1985	Birmingham	Paignton	1V58	2215GgcPgn	
119	37165		Sa	24	8	1985	Paignton	Birmingham	1M86	1000PgnLvp	
120	37061		Fr	30	8	1985	Plymouth	Leeds	1E50	1100PlyLds	
121	37247		Sa	?	9	1985	Par	Plymouth	1A85	1610PnzPad	+500??
122	37239		Th	10	10	1985	Bristol	Plymouth	1Z90	1736BtmPly	vice 0730AbdPnz
123	37185		Tu	29	10	1985	Bristol	Exeter	1C09	0635BtmPly	+50032(T)
124	37222		We	6	11	1985	Largin	Plymouth	1A85	1617PnzPad	+50046(DIT)
125	37222		We	20	11	1985	Largin	Plymouth	1S71	0730PnzAbd	+50039(DIT)
126	37158		Fr	22	11	1985	Bristol	Exeter	1C09	0635BtmPly	+50003(T)
127	37235		Tu	21	1	1986	Bristol	Exeter	1C09	0635BtmPly	+47415(T)

Log	Loco	†	dy		date		from	to	code	train	notes
128	37101		Fr	31	1	1986	Bristol	Exeter	1C09	0635BtmPly	+50031(T)
129	37078		Tu	11	2	1986	Bristol	Exeter	1C09	0635BtmPly	+50012(T)
130	37232		Fr	14	2	1986	Bristol	Exeter	1C09	0635BtmPly	+47431(T)
131	37196		Sa	22	2	1986	Par	Penzance	1V76	0936LvpPnz	+50010(DIT)
132	37204		Tu	4	3	1986	Bristol	Exeter	1C09	0635BtmPly	+47501(T)
133	37195		Th	13	3	1986	Penzance	Plymouth	2C86	1527PnzPly	+47438(DIT)
134	37219		Tu	18	3	1986	Bristol	Exeter	1C09	0635BtmExd	+50046(T)
135	37232		Fr	21	3	1986	Bristol	Exeter	1C09	0635BtmP y	+50035(T)
136	37158		Tu	25	3	1986	Bristol	Exeter	1C09	0635BtmP y	+50002(T)
137	37208		Tu	15	4	1986	Bristol	Exeter	1C09	0635BtmP y	+50049(T)
138	37204		Th	22	5	1986	Treverrin tunnel	Plymouth	1E91	0933PnzNcl	+50044(DIT)
139	37207		Th	5	6	1986	Newton Abbot	Plymouth	1V65	0943NclPnz	
140	37204		Sa	14	6	1986	Par	Plymouth		2105ParPly	50018 in diagram but failed
141	37155		We	23	7	1986	Bodmin Parkway	Plymouth	1S71	0730PnzAbd	propelling 50050(DIT)
142	37155		Sa	30	8	1986	Newton Abbot?	Plymouth	1V64	1200LvpPnz	+47095(DIT)
143	37181		Su	31	8	1986	Truro	Falmouth		....TruFal	+DMU
144	37181		Su	31	8	1986	Falmouth	Truro		....FalTru	+DMU
145	37181		Su	31	8	1986	Truro	Falmouth		....TruFal	+DMU
146	37181		Su	31	8	1986	Falmouth	Truro		....FalTru	+DMU
147	37235	†	Mo	3	11	1986	Largin	Plymouth	1S71	0730PnzAbd	
148	37175-37207	†	We	26	11	1986	Lostwithiel	Plymouth	1A50	1000PnzPad	
149	37199	†	Fr	19	12	1986	Liskeard	Lostwithiel	1C11	0645SdnPnz	+500xx ?
150	37199		Tu	13	1	1987	St Austell	Penzance	1C02	2359PadPnz	+50038
151	37199		Tu	13	1	1987	Penzance	Plymouth	2C83	1200PnzPly	
152	37207		Sa	7	2	1987	Liskeard	Penzance	1C11	0645SdnPnz	+50033(DIT)
153	37207		Sa	7	2	1987	Penzance	Par	1F84	1412PnzBtm	
154	37427	†	Tu	17	2	1987	Bristol	Exeter	1C09	0635BtmPly	
155	37217		Fr	6	3	1987	Bristol	Exeter	1C09	0635BtmPly	+50043(T)
156	37235		Fr	20	3	1987	Lostwithiel	Plymouth	2C84	1200PnzPly	+50006(DIT)
157	37235	†	We	25	3	1987	Plymouth	Penzance	2C74	1635PlyPnz	
158	37235	†	Sa	11	4	1987	Penzance	Plymouth		1626PnzPly	
159	37013		Su	26	4	1987	York	Exeter	1V05	1445YrkPly	term Exeter

Log	Loco	†	dy		date		from	to	code	train	notes
160	37694		Sa	16	5	1987	Wolverhampton	Paignton	1V71	1020GgcPgn	
161	37235	†	We	10	6	1987	Penzance	Plymouth	2C83	0911PnzPly	
162	37675		Sa	20	6	1987	Par	Plymouth	1M62	1005NqyMcp	+4715¢ DIT
163	37674	†	We	1	7	1987	Truro	Plymouth	2C89	1950PnzPly	
164	37250		Sa	4	7	1987	Exeter	Paignton	1V29	2250GgcPgn	
165	37250		Sa	4	7	1987	Paignton	Exeter	1S64	1015PgnGgc	
166	37671		We	15	7	1987	Bristol	Exeter	1C80	2235BtmExd	
167	37207		We	22	7	1987	Penzance	Par	1F88	1830PnzBtm	47373 Par-Plymouth
168	37131+37207		Sa	1	8	1987	Par	Plymouth	1M45	1133 PnzLvp	+47447 DIT
169	37214		Tu	4	8	1987	Cheltenham	Plymouth	1V68	1125NclPnz	+HST
170	37674	†	Sa	29	8	1987	Par	Penzance	1V53	0816LvpPnz	+47515(DIT)
171	37175		Th	3	9	1987	Exeter	Barnstaple	1C07	0405ExdBpl	
172	37175		Th	3	9	1987	Barnstaple	Exeter	2C68	0545BplPnz	
173	37175		Fr	4	9	1987	Exeter	Barnstaple	1C07	0405ExdBpl	
174	37175		Fr	4	9	1987	Barnstaple	Exeter	2C68	0545BplPnz	
175	37175		Sa	5	9	1987	Kings Nympton	Exeter	2B75	1352BplExd	+31464(DIT)
176	37207	†	Fr	18	9	1987	Truro	Plymouth	2C89	1950PnzPly	+500xx¨(DIT)
177	37207		Fr	2	10	1987	Exeter	Barnstaple	1C07	0405ExdBpl	
178	37207		Fr	2	10	1987	Barnstaple	Exeter	2C68	0545BplPnz	
179	37670	†	Fr	23	10	1987	Liskeard	Penzance	1V59	0720GgcPnz	
180	37670	†	Tu	10	11	1987	Largin	Plymouth	1F88	1830PnzBtm	+500xx ˮ
181	37670	†	Tu	10	11	1987	Par	Plymouth	1A02	2135PnzPad	+500xx ˮ
182	37673		Th	12	11	1987	Plymouth	Newton Abbot	1A02	2135PnzPad	+47427(ˮ)
183	37426		Th	19	11	1987	Bristol	Exeter	1C80	2235BtmExd	
184	37672	†	Mo	7	12	1987	Truro	Plymouth	1F88	1830PnzBtm	+500xx ˮ
185	37142		Mo	21	12	1987	Exeter	Plymouth		0657NclPly	+HST
186	37142		Mo	21	12	1987	Plymouth	Bristol		1450PlyYrk	+HST
187	37142		Tu	26	1	1988	Exeter	Paignton	2C20	1745ExmPgn	
188	37142		Tu	26	1	1988	Paignton	Exeter	2C51	1917PgnExd	
189	37673	†	Sa	20	2	1988	St Austell	Penzance	2C68	0702ExdPnz	
190	37673	†	Sa	20	2	1988	Penzance	Plymouth	2C84	1213PnzPly	
191	37674	†	Fr	26	2	1988	Truro	Penzance	1V59	0720GgcPnz	

Log	Loco	†	dy		date	year	from	to	code	train	notes
192	3762	+	Mo	29	2	1988	Newton Abbot	Exeter	2C37	0817PgnExc	+HST 43127/43003
193	3707		Th	17	3	1988	Exeter	Plymouth		1445PadPly	
194	3723		Th	24	3	1988	Honiton	Exeter	1V12	1203PshPgr	
195	3723	+	Fr	6	5	1988	Yeovil Jn	Exeter	1V19	1910WloExd	
196	3764	+	Su	5	6	1988	Truro	Par	1S87	1055PnzAbd	+HST
197	3762	+	Sa	16	7	1988	Truro	Plymouth	1E36	1117PnzNcl	+?
198	37673+37674	+	Su	31	7	1988	Newton Abbot	Plymouth		2140PadPly	+HST
199	37669+37674		Fr	12	8	1988	Exeter	Plymouth	1V54	1325LvpPly	+47606 DIT
200	3765		Sa	27	8	1988	Par	Newquay	1V59	0700GgcNcy	+HST
201	37-11	+	Mo	19	9	1988	Pewsey	Exeter	1C45	1302PadPly	
202	3765		Fr	21	10	1988	Exeter	Plymouth	1V50	0850GgcPrz	+47478(T)
203	37-39	+	Mo	6	2	1989	Axminster	Yeovil Jn	1V11	1100ExdWlo	
204	37-39		Mo	6	2	1989	Chard Jn	Axminster	1V13	1310WloExd	propelling 33118
205	37671-37675	+	Sa	1	4	1989	Par	Plymouth		1730PnzBtm	
206	3763		Sa	27	5	1989	Par	Newquay		0915PlyNqy	+HST
207	3763		Sa	27	5	1989	Newquay	Exeter	1A61	1105NqyPad	+HST
208	3764	+	Sa	27	5	1989	Par	Newquay	1C38	1205PadNqy	+HST
209	3714	+	We	31	5	1989	Plymouth	Exeter	1A02	2045PnzPad	+?
210	3712	+	Sa	3	6	1989	Par	Newquay		....PadNqy	+HST
211	3748	+	Mo	26	6	1989	Exeter	Plymouth		2200PadPly	+HST
212	3767C+37671	+	Sa	12	8	1989	Truro	Plymouth	1S71	0817PnzGgc	+HST
213	3764		Sa	19	8	1989	Par	Penzance		1025PadPnz	+HST
214	3764		Sa	19	8	1989	Penzance	Exeter		1620PnzPad	+HST
215	3767C+37672		Sa	26	8	1989	Bodmin Parkway	Exeter	1A44	0735PnzPad	+HST
216	3764	+	Th	31	8	1989	Par	Plymouth		1630PnzPad	+HST
217	3764		Sa	7	10	1989	Penzance	Plymouth		0827PnzPad	+HST
218	3765		Sa	14	10	1989	Plymouth	Exeter		0815PlyYrk	+HST
219	3765		Sa	21	10	1989	Penzance	Exeter	1A56	0955PnzFad	+HST
220	3757		Su	29	10	1989	Newton Abbot?	Plymouth	1C28	0940PadPnz	+HST - term Plymouth
221	3757		Mo	30	10	1989	Plymouth	Exeter	1A03	2145PnzPad	+47587(T)
222	3767-1	+	Th	25	1	1990	Newton Abbot	Exeter		1800NabExd	
223	3741-+37670		We	7	2	1990	Exeter	Plymouth	1C54	1635PadPly	+HST

Log	Loco	†	dy	date			from	to	code	train	notes
224	37215		Tu	27	2	1990	Exeter	Plymouth		1618McpPly	
225	37673		Fr	20	4	1990	Bristol	Exeter		1722BtmExd	
226	37674	†	Sa	7	7	1990	Par	Penzance	1C02	2359PadPnz	
227	37672		Sa	7	7	1990	Newquay?	Exeter		0815NqyMcp	+HST 43112/072
228	37669		Sa	21	7	1990	Par	Bristol	1S04	1000PnzEdb	
229	37414		Fr?	3	8	1990	Par?	Plymouth		1330PnzPly?	+DMU
230	37414		Sa	4	8	1990	Par	Plymouth		1440PnzMcp	+47852
231	37671		Sa	18	8	1990	Par	Exeter	1A58	1130NqyPad	+HST
232	37191		Fr	9	11	1990	Exeter	Salisbury	1Z40	1505ExdSal	
233	37675	†	Sa	8	12	1990	Par	Exeter		0930PnzEdb	
234	37158		Su	9	12	1990	Exeter	Plymouth	1C44	1235PadPnz	+HST
235	37158		Mo	24	12	1990	Exeter	Honiton	2B81	1707PlmHon	vice DMU
236	37158		Mo	24	12	1990	Honiton	Exeter	2B84	1905HonExd	vice DMU
237	37158		Mo	7	1	1991	Paignton	Exeter		1444PgnExd	vice 1444PgnNcl
238	37146		Tu	22	1	1991	Exeter	Barnstaple	2B76	1515ExdBpl	with 3 Mk1
239	37146		Tu	22	1	1991	Barnstaple	Exeter	2B77	1618BplExd	with 3 Mk1
240	37146		We	23	1	1991	Exeter Central	Barnstaple	2B78	1605ExcBpl	+DMU
241	37146		We	23	1	1991	Barnstaple	Exeter	2B83	1746BplExd	+DMU
242	37146		Fr	25	1	1991	Exeter	Barnstaple	2B76	1515ExdBpl	+DMU
243	37146		Fr	25	1	1991	Barnstaple	Exeter	2B77	1618BplExd	+DMU
244	37146		Fr	25	1	1991	Exeter	Barnstaple	2B80	1736ExdBpl	+DMU
245	37146		Fr	25	1	1991	Barnstaple	Exeter	2B85	1925BplExd	+DMU
246	37359	†	Tu	29	1	1991	Lostwithiel	Penzance	1C02	2355PadPnz	+47xxx
247	37411		Fr	8	2	1991	Exeter	Plymouth	1Z33	0752ExdPly	vice 2055EdbPly
248	37411		Sa	9	2	1991	Exeter	Plymouth	2C66	0915ExdPnz	
249	37054	†	We	20	2	1991	Exeter	Plymouth	1V56	1142NclPnz	+HST
250	37054		Sa	23	2	1991	Exeter	Bristol	1A03	2215PnzPad	+47817(?)
251	37098	†	Mo	4	3	1991	Exeter	Bristol	1S85	0710PlyEdb	+HST
252	37083		Mo	11	3	1991	Exeter	Plymouth	1C54	1635PadPly	+HST
253	37098		Su	17	3	1991	Exeter	Plymouth		1555NclPly	+HST
254	37675		Mo	18	3	1991	Par	Penzance		1935PadPnz	+HST
255	37083		We	20	3	1991	Plymouth	Birmingham	1S71	0716PnzAbd	+47810

Log	t	Loco	dy	date			from	to	code	train	notes
256		37141	We	3	4	1991	Exeter Central	Barnstaple	2B80	1730ExcBpl	
257		37141	We	3	4	1991	Barnstaple	Exeter	2B85	1925BplExd	
258		37174	We	1	5	1991	Exeter	Yeovil Jn	2O04	1737ExdWlo	banking at rear
259		37135	Th	16	5	1991	Exeter St.Davids	Exeter Central	1A03	2215PnzPad	+HST
260		37146	Mo	20	5	1991	Westbury	Exeter	1C66	1835PadPly	+DMU
261		37010	Fr	24	5	1991	Exeter	Barnstaple	2B74	1257ExdBpl	+DMU
262		37010	Fr	24	5	1991	Barnstaple	Exeter Central	2F19	1414BplExd	+DMU
263		37010	Fr	24	5	1991	Exeter Central	Barnstaple	2B78	1605ExcBpl	+DMU
264		37010	Fr	24	5	1991	Barnstaple	Exeter	2B83	1746BplExd	+HST
265		37135	Mo	27	5	1991	Exeter	Plymouth	1C32	1135PadPly	+HST
266		37135	Mo	27	5	1991	Exeter	Plymouth	1C66	1835PadPly	+47xxx(DIT)
267		37207	Sa	1	6	1991	Newton Abbot	Plymouth	1V32	2055GgcPly	47827 failed
268		37138	Sa	1	6	1991	Exeter	Paddington	1A52	1130PgnPad	+47801. 78 mins late
269		37010	Fr	7	6	1991	Dainton	Plymouth	1V46	0918McpPly	+50002
270		37135	Mo	10	6	1991	Honiton	Exeter	1V17	1655WloExd	+50037(DIT)
271		37141	We	19	6	1991	Yeovil Jn ?	Exeter	2V13	1315WloExd	+HST
272		37097	Su	7	7	1991	Totnes	Exeter	1M62	0855PlyMcp	+HST
273		37054	Su	7	7	1991	Exeter	Plymouth	1C62	1635PadPly	+HST
274		37097	Su	7	7	1991	Exeter	Plymouth	1V62	1610McpPly	+HST
275		37063	Su	7	7	1991	Exeter	Plymouth	1C76	1935PadPnz	+HST
276		37141	Sa	19	6	1991	Crewkerne	Exeter	2V13	1315WloExd	+50037
277		37141	Sa	20	7	1991	Paignton	Exeter	1M78	1216PgnMcp	47845 forward
278		37141	Tu	23	7	1991	Exeter	Plymouth	1V48	1016LvpPly	+HST
279		37141	Tu	23	7	1991	Plymouth	Bristol	1E39	1710PlyLcs	+HST
280		37207	Sa	27	7	1991	Paignton	Bristol	1M10	1705PgnMcp	
281		37098	Mo	29	7	1991	Exeter	Plymouth	1V48	1016LvpPly	+HST
282		37098	Mo	29	7	1991	Plymouth	Exeter	1E39	1710PlyLds	+HST
283		37010	Sa	10	8	1991	Exeter	Plymouth	2C13	0800ExmPly	+DMU
284		37254	Sa	10	8	1991	Lavington	Penzance	1C27	1030PadPnz	+HST
285		37098	Tu	13	8	1991	Exeter	Newton Abbot	2C13	0800ExmNab	to be confirmed
286		37098	Mo	19	8	1991	Exeter	Plymouth	1V52	0944GgcPnz	+HST
287		37010	Tu	20	8	1991	Newton Abbot	Plymouth	1C44	1435PadPnz	+HST

Log	Loco	†	dy	date			from	to	code	train	notes
288	37258		Fr	23	8	1991	Totnes (Rattery)	Plymouth		0735PadPly	+HST(propelling)
289	37258		Fr	23	8	1991	Plymouth	Waterloo	1O40	1355PlyWlo	
290	37258		Fr	23	8	1991	Waterloo	Exeter	2V21	1915WloExd	
291	37098		Sa	24	8	1991	Exeter	Paignton	1V41	0720NtmPgn	+HST
292	37098		Sa	24	8	1991	Paignton	Exeter	1M86	1345PgnNtm	+HST
293	37098		Sa	24	8	1991	Exeter	Newton Abbot	1V49	0752NclPgn	+HST
294	37098		We	28	8	1991	Exeter	Plymouth	1V56	1205NclPly	+HST
295	37098		Fr	30	8	1991	Plymouth	Exeter	1A70	1236PnzPad	+4782↲
296	37372		We	4	9	1991	Exeter	Bristol	1S19	2100PlyEdb	
297	37419		Fr	6	9	1991	Exeter	Yeovil Jn	2O04	1738ExdWlo	
298	37419		Su	8	9	1991	Exeter	Basingstoke	2O05	2040ExdBsk	+HST
299	37191		Tu	10	9	1991	Exeter	Plymouth	1C12	0745PadPnz	+HST
300	37258		Su	22	9	1991	Exeter	Bristol	1S19	2100PlyEdb	+47xx?
301	37158		Mo	23	9	1991	Exeter	Plymouth	1V35	0605DbyPly	+4782↲
302	37158		Mo	23	9	1991	Plymouth	Exeter	1M56	1203PlyMcp	+4782↲
303	37158	†	Th	26	9	1991	Dawlish	Plymouth	1C28	1035PadPnz	+HST
304	37098		Sa	28	9	1991	Exeter	Bristol	1A03	2135PnzPad	+4784E(DIT)
305	37411	†	Sa	28	9	1991	Totnes	Plymouth	1V33	2120GgcPly	(propelling)
306	37412		Sa	28	9	1991	Par	Exeter		0940NqyEdb	+HST
307	37098		Su	29	9	1991	Exeter	Salisbury	2O03	1722ExdWlo	
308	37098		Su	29	9	1991	Salisbury	Exeter	1V19	1855WloExd	
309	37133		Fr	1	11	1991	Exeter	Gloucester	2B18	1540ExdGlr	+DMU
310	37417+37420	†	We	6	11	1991	Bodmin Parkway	Plymouth	1A48	0847PnzPad	
311	37133		Su	10	11	1991	Honiton	Exeter	1VO8	0745BskExd	
312	37142		Sa	23	11	1991	Plymouth	Paddington	1A61	1335PlyPad	+HST
313	37141		Th	28	11	1991	Exeter	Plymouth	1V48	1016LvpPly	+HST
314	37142		Th	28	11	1991	Honiton	Exeter	1V11	1115WloExd	
315	37670		Sa	14	12	1991	Par	Plymouth		1905PnzPly	+HST
316	37673		Su	15	12	1991	Hemerdon	Bristol	1S91	1308PlmEdb	+HST
317	37010		We	15	1	1992	Exeter	Waterloo	2O02	1422ExdWlo	
318	37207		Su	2	2	1992	Exeter	Plymouth	1C34	1020PadPnz	+HST
319	37372		We	19	2	1992	Exeter	Basingstoke	1O44	1940ExdBsk	+47701(CIT)

Log	Loco	†	dy		date		from	to	code	train	notes
320	37237		Fr	21	2	1992	Exeter	Newton Abbot	2C59	2210ExdNab	
321	37237		Sa	22	2	1992	Exeter	Plymouth	1V38	0605LdsPly	+HST
322	37237		Sa	22	2	1992	Exeter	Salisbury	1O41	1622ExdWlo	
323	37263		Mo	2	3	1992	Exeter	Plymouth	1V53	2120GgcPly	+47836(T)
324	37097		We	4	3	1992	Exeter	Plymouth	1C02	0005PadPnz	
325	37263		Fr	6	3	1992	Exeter	Bristol	1A03	2215PnzPad	
326	37038		Mo	13	4	1992	Exeter	Salisbury	2O02	1422ExdWlo	
327	37038		Mo	13	4	1992	Salisbury	Exeter	1V17	1655WloExd	
328	37010		Th	16	4	1992	Exeter	Yeovil Jn	2O04	1738ExdWlo	
329	37010		Th	16	4	1992	Yeovil Jn	Exeter	1V17	1655WloExd	
330	37038		Mo	20	4	1992	Axminster	Exeter	1V19	1855WloExd	+47707(DIT)
331	37038		Tu	21	4	1992	Newton Abbot	Exeter	2C08	0712NabExd	+47599
332	37010		Tu	21	4	1992	Exeter	Salisbury	1O31	0611ExdWlo	
333	37010		Tu	21	4	1992	Salisbury	Exeter	1V11	1100WloExd	+33102(DIT)
334	37010	†	Th	30	4	1992	Exeter	Plymouth	1C12	0745PadPnz	+HST
335	37230		Fr	1	5	1992	Exeter	Plymouth	1C44	1435PadPnz	+HST
336	37412	†	Fr	15	5	1992	Truro	Plymouth	1A91	1630PnzPad	+HST
337	37230	†	Sa	16	5	1992	Par	Plymouth	1C51	1935PnzPly	+HST
338	37010		We	20	5	1992	Westbury	Exeter	1C36	1235PadPnz	+HST (term Exd)
339	37230		Fr	22	5	1992	Cowley Bridge	Exeter	1V59	0912AbdPnz	
340	37010		Tu	26	5	1992	Exeter	Salisbury	1O41	1622ExdWlo	
341	37010		Tu	26	5	1992	Salisbury	Exeter	1V19	1815WloExd	
342	37141	†	Th	28	5	1992	Exeter	Plymouth	1C12	0745PadPnz	+HST
343	37010	†	Tu	2	6	1992	Exeter	Plymouth	1C02	2355PadPnz	
344	37092		Th	11	6	1992	Exeter	Bristol	1M48	1548PlyDby	
345	37230		Sa	13	6	1992	Crewkerne	Exeter	1V10	1047BskPgn	+47579(T)
346	37671-37675		Sa	13	6	1992	Exeter	Plymouth	1V47	1018McpPnz	+HST
347	37671-37675		Su	14	6	1992	Exeter	Plymouth	1C72	1835PadPly	+HST
348	37411	†	Sa	20	6	1992	Lostwithiel	Penzance		2115NclFnz	+HST
349	37572		Su	21	6	1992	Exeter	Paignton	1Z22	0800PadPgn	gala relief
350	37672		Su	21	6	1992	Paignton	Exeter	1Z22	1805PgnPad	gala relief
351	37054		Mo	22	6	1992	Exeter	Plymouth	1V48	1015LvpPly	+HST

Log	Loco	†	dy	date			from	to	code	train	notes
352	37054		Mo	22	6	1992	Plymouth	Exeter	1E39	1710PlyLds	+1ST
353	37230		Mo	22	6	1992	Topsham	Exeter		1850ExmExd	DMU P824
354	37054	†	Sa	27	6	1992	Exeter	Plymouth	1C02	0005PadPnz	+47xxx
355	37230		Sa	4	7	1992	Paignton	Bristol	1S93	1530PgnGgc	
356	37230		Sa	4	7	1992	Exeter	Taunton	1A91	1638PnzPad	+1ST, term Tnt
357	37230		Th	9	7	1992	Exeter	Salisbury	1O41	1622ExdWlo	
358	37230		Th	9	7	1992	Salisbury	Exeter	1V19	1815WloExd	
359	37411	†	Fr	17	7	1992	Menheniot	Penzance	1C02	0005PadPnz	
360	37670+37672		Sa	8	8	1992	Par	Newquay	1V37?	0655McpNqy	+1ST
361	37672+37670		Sa	8	8	1992	Newquay	Plymouth	1E44	1440NqyLds	+37672(M)+HST. 110 late
362	37230		Mo	10	8	1992	Crewkerne	Exeter	1V09	0835WloExd	
363	37054		Mo	10	8	1992	Exeter	Plymouth	1C50	1535PadPnz	+1ST
364	37413+37675		Sa	22	8	1992	Par	Newquay	1V26	2355LdsNqy	+1ST
365	37675+37413		Sa	22	8	1992	Newquay	Par	1M62	0815NqyMcp	+1ST
366	37672		Sa	22	8	1992	Par	Exeter	1M62	0815NqyMcp	
367	37886		Sa	29	8	1992	Exeter	Bristol	1S66	1037PgnGgc	+47814(T)
368	37054		Su	30	8	1992	Exeter	Plymouth	1C17	1025BtmPly	
369	37054		Mo	31	8	1992	Tiverton Pkwy	Taunton	1E29	0625PlyNcl	+1ST(propelling)
370	37671		Mo	7	9	1992	Chard Jn	Exeter	1V19	1815WloExd	
371	37372		Su	13	9	1992	Exeter	Salisbury	1O41	1607ExdWlo	
372	37372		Su	13	9	1992	Salisbury	Exeter	1V19	1855WloExd	+47583(DIT)
373	37141		Mo	12	10	1992	Exeter	Plymouth	1V52	0944GgcPnz	+1ST
374	37197		Tu	27	10	1992	Plymouth	Exeter		064PnzZPad	+HST
375	37141		Tu	27	10	1992	Exeter	Salisbury	1O41	1622ExdWlo	
376	37141		Tu	27	10	1992	Salisbury	Exeter	1V19	1815WloExd	
377	37141		Th	29	10	1992	Exeter	Salisbury	1O41	1622ExdWlo	
378	37141		Th	29	10	1992	Salisbury	Exeter	1V19	1815WloExd	47708(DIT)
379	37141		Su	1	11	1992	Exeter	Plymouth	1C56	1535PadPnz	+HST
380	37012		We	11	11	1992	Exeter	Plymouth	1C22	0945PadPly	+HST
381	37054		Fr	20	11	1992	Feniton	Exeter	1V15	1515WloExd	+47712
382	37010		Mo	30	11	1992	Truro	Bristol	1S35	0925PnzEdb	+HST
383	37098		Th	3	12	1992	Exeter	Plymouth		0950GgcPnz	+HST

Log	Loco	†	dy	date			from	to	code	train	notes
384	37098		Su	6	12	1992	Exeter	Salisbury	1O35	0928ExdWlo	
385	37098		Su	6	12	1992	Salisbury	Exeter	1V11	1055WloExd	+33114(T)
386	37054		Su	6	12	1992	Exeter	Plymouth	1C72	1835PadPly	+HST
387	37054		Tu	8	12	1992	Exeter	Waterloo	1O41	1622ExdWlo	
388	37054		We	9	12	1992	Exeter	Plymouth	1V59	0900AbdPly	+HST
389	37092		Sa	12	12	1992	Axminster	Exeter	2V05	0615SalExd	+47710
390	37092	†	We	23	12	1992	Exeter	Plymouth	1V56	1205NclPly	+HST
391	37092		Tu	5	1	1993	Exeter	Reading	1A03	2215PnzPad	+478xx
392	37197		Su	10	1	1993	Exeter	Plymouth	1C56	1535PadPnz	+HST
393	37197		Su	10	1	1993	Exeter	Plymouth	1V58	1125EdbPnz	+HST
394	37258		Sa	23	1	1993	Exeter	Salisbury		0811ExdBsk	
395	37258		Sa	23	1	1993	Salisbury	Exeter	1V09	0915WloExd	+47709(DIT)
396	37411		Sa	23	1	1993	Exeter	Basingstoke	1O37	1225ExdBsk	
397	37411		Sa	23	1	1993	Basingstoke	Exeter	1V17	1802BskExd	
398	37258		Tu	26	1	1993	Taunton	Plymouth	1V59	0912AbdPly	+HST
399	37258	†	We	27	1	1993	Exeter	Plymouth		1145PadPnz	+HST
400	37197		Su	7	2	1993	Exeter	Plymouth	1C53	1508RdgPnz	+HST
401	37258		Tu	9	2	1993	Crewkerne	Exeter	2V13	1315WloExd	+47706(DIT)
402	37197		We	17	2	1993	Exeter	Plymouth	1C60	1735PadPnz	+HST
403	37146		Tu	2	3	1993	Exeter	Salisbury	1O35	0945ExdWlo	
404	37146		Tu	2	3	1993	Salisbury	Exeter	1V11	1115WloExd	
405	37197		Th	4	3	1993	Gillingham	Exeter	1V11	1115WloExd	
406	37227		Su	21	3	1993	Exeter	Penzance	1C53	1415PadPnz	+HST
407	37146		Mo	22	3	1993	Exeter	Salisbury	1O41	1622ExdWlo	
408	37146		Mo	22	3	1993	Salisbury	Exeter	1V19	1815WloExd	+47714
409	37098		Th	25	3	1993	Honiton ?	Exeter	1V15	1515WloExd	+47714
410	37140		Sa	3	4	1993	Woking	Exeter	2V21	1915WloExd	
411	37012		Mo	5	4	1993	Exeter	Plymouth	1C32	1135PadPly	+HST
412	37141		Sa	17	4	1993	Newton Abbot	Exeter	1S85	0725PlyAbd	+HST
413	37046		Mo	26	4	1993	Exeter	Basingstoke	1O41	1622ExdWlo	
414	37174		Sa	29	5	1993	Paignton	Exeter	1S93	1518PgnGgc	47714 forward
415	37174		Sa	29	5	1993	Exeter	Plymouth	1C54	1635PadPly	+HST

Log	Loco	†	dy	date			from	to	code	train	notes
416	37174		Fr	11	6	1993	Crewkerne	Exeter	1V17	1730WloExd	+47717(DIT)
417	37042		Su	13	6	1993	Totnes	Bristol		0835PlyPad	+HST
418	37092+37158+37197		Su	20	6	1993	Paddington	Paignton	1Z60	0840PadPgn	gala relief
419	37158+37092+37197		Su	20	6	1993	Paignton	Paddington	1Z60	1740PgnPad	gala relief
420	37191		Su	27	6	1993	Newton Abbot	Exeter		1242PnzPad	+HST
421	37174	†	Tu	29	6	1993	Exeter	Plymouth	1C22	0945PadPly	+HST
422	37191		Fr	2	7	1993	Exeter	Plymouth	1V49	0945YrkPly	+47839(DIT)
423	37035		Mo	5	7	1993	Newton Abbot	Bristol	1M40	1144PlyLvp	+47850
424	37035		Sa	10	7	1993	Exeter	Bristol		0955PgnMcp	+47594(DIT)
425	37174		We	11	8	1993	Westbury	Plymouth	1C32	1135PadPly	+HST
426	37174		We	11	8	1993	Exeter	Plymouth	1V59	0900AbdPly	+HST
427	37223	†	We	25	8	1993	Taunton	Plymouth	1V33	2300GgcPly	+47818(DIT)
428	37109		We	1	9	1993	Exeter	Plymouth	1C44	1435PadPnz	+HST
429	37054	†	Sa	11	9	1993	Exeter	Plymouth		2330LdsNqy	+HST
430	37054		Sa	18	9	1993	Exeter	Plymouth	1V47	1018McpPnz	+HST
431	37263		Sa	18	9	1993	Paignton	Bristol	1M42	1611PgnLvp	
432	37077		Sa	25	9	1993	Dawlish Warren	Plymouth	1V35	0605DbyPnz	+HST
433	37038		Sa	25	9	1993	Paignton	Bristol	1M42	1611PgnLvp	+47815(T)
434	37675		Tu	28	9	1993	Largin	Plymouth		1445PnzPad	+HST(propelling)
435	37203		Tu	28	9	1993	Exeter	Plymouth	1V48	1018LvpPly	+HST
436	37203		Tu	28	9	1993	Plymouth	Bristol	1E39	1700PlyLds	+HST
437	37219		Sa	2	10	1993	Newton Abbot	Bristol	1S93	1518PgnGgc	+47596
438	37012		We	3	11	1993	Exeter	Plymouth	1C12	0745PadPnz	+HST
439	37012		We	3	11	1993	Plymouth	Exeter	1A54	0942PnzPad	+HST
440	37012		We	3	11	1993	Exeter	Plymouth	1C32	1135PadPly	+HST
441	37040		Tu	9	11	1993	Exeter	Plymouth	1V48	1018LvpPly	+HST
442	37222		Tu	9	11	1993	Exeter	Plymouth	1C32	1235PadPnz	+HST
443	37038		Fr	12	11	1993	Exeter	Bristol	1M56	1015PlyMcp	+47826+47845
444	37408		Tu	23	12	1993	Westbury	Exeter	1C02	2355PadPnz	via Yeovil+Honiton
445	37038		Sa	8	1	1994	Exeter	Plymouth	1C22	0835PadPly	+HST
446	37038		Sa	8	1	1994	Plymouth	Exeter	1A61	1335PlyPad	+HST
447	37418		Tu	11	1	1994	Bristol	Paignton	1C21	1000CdfPgn	

Log	_oco	†	dy		date	1994	from	to	code	train	notes
448	37418		Tu	11	1	1994	Paignton	Bristol	1B40	1345PgnCdf	
449	37040		Th	27	1	1994	Exeter	Plymouth		0935PadPly	+HST
450	37174		Fr	11	2	1994	Exeter	Plymouth	1V56	1205NclPly	+HST
451	37174		Su	13	2	1994	Exeter	Bristol	1S19	2100PlyGgc	+47717
452	37422		Tu	15	2	1994	Bristol	Paignton	1C21	1048BtnPgn	
453	37422		Tu	15	2	1994	Paignton	Bristol	1B40	1340PgnBtm	
454	37412	†	Th	17	2	1994	Par	Penzance	1C02	2355PadPnz	+47818
455	37077		Tu	22	2	1994	Exeter	Plymouth	1C54	1635PadPly	+HST
456	37219		Fr	25	2	1994	Exeter	Penzance	1C40	1335PadPnz	+HST
457	37213		Sa	5	3	1994	Exeter	Bristol	1M56	1015PlyMcp	+47853
458	37097		Su	27	3	1994	Exeter	Plymouth	1C66	1735PadPnz	+HST
459	37077		Tu	29	3	1994	Exeter	Plymouth	1C82	2035PadPly	+HST
460	37038		Tu	5	4	1994	Exeter	Reading	1A54	0942PnzPad	+HST term Reading
461	37264		Fr	8	4	1994	Exeter	Plymouth	1V56	1205NclPly	+HST
462	37191		Tu	17	5	1994	Exeter	Bristol	1S19	2045PlyGgc	+47848
463	37191		Fr	3	6	1994	Exeter	Plymouth	1C54	1635PadPly	+HST
464	37146		Sa	11	6	1994	Exeter	Plymouth	1C76	1930PadPly	+HST
465	37213		Sa	25	6	1994	Exeter	Paignton	1V46	0605GgcPgn	
466	37213		Sa	25	6	1994	Paignton	Bristol	1M48	1603PgnLvp	
467	37038		Th	30	6	1994	Exeter	Bristol	1M40	1144PlyLvp	+47844(DIT)
468	37141		Fr	8	7	1994	Exeter	Bristol	1A24	0640ExdPad	+HST
469	37263	†	Mo	11	7	1994	Exeter	Plymouth	1C02	2355PadPnz	+47847 (DIT)
470	37263	†	Mo	11	7	1994	Ivybridge	Totnes		0735PlyPad	+HST
471	37254		Th	14	7	1994	Totnes	Plymouth	1C76	1935PadPly	+HST
472	37263		Sa	16	7	1994	Exeter	Paignton	1V50	1217McpPgn	+HST
473	37416		We	10	8	1994	Par	Penzance		0005PadPnz	+47810 (DIT)
474	37142+37258		Sa	13	8	1994	Exeter	Reading	1A16	0643ExdRdg	+HST
475	37258		Tu	23	8	1994	Exeter	Bristol	1Z37	1448NabBtm	vice 1430 Paignton-Newcastle
476	37191		Th	1	9	1994	Exeter	Exminster??		0835BtmPly	+HST(drag back-hit cows)
477	37207	†	Mo	5	9	1994	Exeter	Bristol		0620PlvNcl	+HST
478	37197		Th	15	9	1994	Exeter	Plymouth		0640DdePnz	+HST
479	37413	†	Th	15	9	1994	Liskeard	Penzance	1C28	1035PadPnz	+HST

Log	Loco	†	dy				†	from	to	code	train	notes
480	37197		Th	6	10	1994		Exeter	Plymouth		0640DdePnz	+HST
481	37254		Tu	18	10	1994		Hackney Yard	Newton Abbot	1V48	1217McpPly	+47840(DIT) term Nab
482	37207		We	19	10	1994		Exeter	Bristol	1M48	1545PlyDby	
483	37141	†	Mo	24	10	1994		Exeter	Plymouth	1C02	2355PadPnz	+47815
484	37158		Tu	25	10	1994		Exeter	Penzance		1735PadPnz	+HST
485	37258	†	Tu	20	12	1994		Exeter	Plymouth	1C22	0945PadPly	+HST
486	37142		Tu	3	1	1995		Exeter	Bristol	1M48	1545PlyDby	+47845(T)
487	37137		Tu	17	1	1995		Exeter	Plymouth	1V38	0605LdsPly	+HST
488	37137		Tu	17	1	1995		Plymouth	Exeter	1E36	1300PlyLds	+HST
489	37158		Th	2	2	1995		Plymouth	Bristol	1S19	2045PlyGgc	+47848(T)
490	37010		Mo	27	2	1995		Cogload Jn	Exeter	1V46	0918LvpPly	+47831
491	37146		Fr	3	3	1995		Exeter	Plymouth	1V63	1500NclPly	+HST
492	37146		Th	16	3	1995		Dainton	Bristol	1E48	1545PlySfd	+47830(DIT)
493	37229		Th	16	3	1995	†	Par	Penzance		1335PadPnz	+HST
494	37258		Sa	18	3	1995		Tiverton Pkwy.	Bristol	1M48	1545PlyDby	+47840(DIT)
495	37141		Mo	27	3	1995		Taunton	Exeter	1V35	0643WvpPly	+47830(DIT)term Exd
496	37141		Mo	27	3	1995		Exeter	Bristol	1M40	1144PlyLvp	+47830(DIT)start Exd
497	37258		Th	13	4	1995		Paignton	Exeter	1E37	1430PgnNcl	+HST
498	37407		Sa	15	4	1995		Cardiff	Paignton	1C21	1000CdfPgn	
499	37407		Sa	15	4	1995		Paignton	Bristol	1B33	1332PgnBtm	
500	37407		Th	20	4	1995		Bristol	Paignton	1C21	1048BtmPgn	
501	37407		Th	20	4	1995		Paignton	Bristol	1B33	1332PgnBtm	
502	37158		Sa	22	4	1995		Paignton	Exeter		1500PgnPad	+HST
503	37178		Th	1	6	1995		Exeter	Plymouth	1V48	1217McpPly	+47830(DIT)
504	37178		Tu	6	6	1995		Plymouth	Penzance	1C50	1535PadPnz	+HST
505	37178		Su	11	6	1995		Exeter	Penzance	1C20	0910PadPnz	+HST
506	37178		Su	11	6	1995		Penzance	Exeter	1A92	1540PnzPad	+HST
507	37158		Mo	12	6	1995		Exeter	Plymouth	1C28	1035PadPnz	+HST
508	37197		Tu	13	6	1995		Taunton	Plymouth	1C32	1135PadPly	+HST
509	37158		Fr	16	6	1995		Exeter	Plymouth	1V35	0604DbyPly	+47844(DIT)
510	37158		Fr	16	6	1995		Plymouth	Bristol	1M40	1144PlyLvp	
511	37158		Fr	16	6	1995		Bristol	Exeter	1V49	0943YrkExd	+HST

Log	loco	†	dy		date	from	to	code	train	notes
512	37158		Fr	23	6	1995	Exeter	Plymouth	1C50	1535PadPnz	+HST
513	37158		Sa	24	6	1995	Exeter	Plymouth	1V30	2004EdbPnz	+HST
514	37197		Th	20	7	1995	Exeter	Penzance	1C12	0745PadPnz	+HST
515	37197		Th	20	7	1995	Penzance	Exeter	1A81	1440PnzPad	+HST
516	37197		Fr	4	8	1995	Exeter	Plymouth	1C22	0945PacPly	+HST
517	37197		Fr	11	8	1995	Exeter	Reading	1A76	1535PlyPad	+HST
518	37141		Sa	12	8	1995	Rewe	Exeter	1V46	0605GgcPgn	47829(DIT)term Exd
519	37197		Fr	18	8	1995	Teignmouth	Plymouth	1V35	0604DbyPly	+47841(DIT)
520	37197		Fr	18	8	1995	Plymouth	Bristol	1M40	1144PlyLvp	+47841(DIT)
521	37197		Fr	18	8	1995	Exeter	Plymouth	1C54	1635PacPly	+HST
522	37213		We	23	8	1995	Exeter	Plymouth	1V38	0605LdsPly	+HST
523	37158		Th	31	8	1995	Exeter	Plymouth	1C66	1835PadPly	+HST
524	37158		Fr	1	9	1995	Exeter	Plymouth	1C28	1035PadPnz	+HST
525	37213		Su	3	9	1995	Exeter	Penzance	1C52	1410PadPnz	+HST
526	37213		We	6	9	1995	Powderham	Exeter	1E40	1650PlySfd	
527	37197		We	20	9	1995	Exeter	Plymouth	1C22	0935PadPly	+HST
528	37672	†	Su	1	10	1995	Par	Penzance	1C50	1535PacPnz	+HST
529	37158		We	18	10	1995	Exeter	Plymouth	1C54	1635PadPly	+HST
530	37158		Fr	20	10	1995	Exeter	Plymouth	1C32	1135PadPly	+HST
531	37521		Tu	7	11	1995	Exeter	Plymouth	1C36	1235PadPnz	+HST
532	37214		Sa	18	11	1995	Exeter	Plymouth	1V39	0605LdsPly	+HST
533	37263		Tu	21	11	1995	Exeter	Plymouth	1V50	0640DdePnz	+HST
534	37263		Tu	21	11	1995	Exeter	Plymouth	1V57	0910AbdPly	+HST
535	37413		Tu	12	12	1995	Bristol	Paignton	1C21	1054BtmPgn	
536	37413		Tu	12	12	1995	Paignton	Bristol	1B33	1332PgnBtm	
537	37229		Sa	30	12	1995	Exeter	Plymouth	1V63	1500NclPly	+HST
538	37229		Mo	1	1	1996	Exeter	Plymouth	1C50	1535PadPnz	+HST
539	37696		We	10	1	1996	Exeter	Penzance	1V52	0850EdbPnz	+HST
540	37695		Sa	13	1	1996	Par	Penzance	1V29	2350WloPnz	
541	37158		Fr	26	1	1996	Exeter	Plymouth	1C82	2035PadPly	+HST
542	37229		Tu	30	1	1996	Exeter	Plymouth	1V29	2350WloPnz	+47815(DIT)
543	37229		Tu	30	1	1996	Exeter	Bristol	1M56	1044PlyMcp	+47575(ETH)

Log	Loco	†	dy		date		from	to	code	train	notes
544	37229		Mo	5	2	1996	Exeter	Plymouth	1V56	0910LvpPly	+47853(DIT)
545	37158		Su	17	3	1996	Exeter	Plymouth	1C66	1310EdbPnz	+HST
546	37671		We	20	3	1996	Bodmin Parkway	Plymouth	1S71	0720PnzEdb	+HST
547	37158		Fr	12	4	1996	Exeter	Plymouth	1C44	1445PadPnz	+HST - term Plymouth
548	37213		We	24	4	1996	Exeter	Plymouth	1C76	1935PadPly	+HST
549	37213		Th	25	4	1996	Plymouth	Exeter	1O03	2215PnzWlo	+47816(T)
550	37254		We	8	5	1996	Bristol	Plymouth	1V48	1217McpPly	+HST
551	37254		Fr	17	5	1996	Exeter	Penzance	1V52	0850EdbPnz	+HST
552	37521		Th	6	6	1996	Exeter	Leeds	1E39	1607ExdLds	+HST
553	37696		Sa	8	6	1996	Probus	Truro	1V47	1017McpPnz	propelling 47814(DIT)
554	37197		We	12	6	1996	Exeter	Plymouth	1C28	1045PadPnz	+HST
555	37670		Sa	15	6	1996	Par	Newquay	1V39	0605LdsNqy	+HST
556	37670		Sa	15	6	1996	Newquay	Par	1E39	1408NqyLds	+HST(propelling)
557	37197		Tu	18	6	1996	Bridgwater	Plymouth	1V29	2350WloPnz	+47811(DIT)
558	37197		Tu	2	7	1996	Exeter	Paddington	1A19	0555PlyPad	+HST
559	37254		Fr	26	7	1996	Exeter	Penzance	1C28	1045PadPnz	+HST
560	37263		Fr	2	8	1996	Exeter	Plymouth	1C36	1235PadPnz	+HST
561	37254		Tu	6	8	1996	Ivybridge	Birmingham	1M56	1044PlyMcp	+47814(DIT)
562	37411		We	14	8	1996	Exeter	Paignton	1Z70	0855ExdPgn	
563	37411		We	14	8	1996	Paignton	Bristol	1Z71	1631PgnBtm	
564	37411		Sa	17	8	1996	Cardiff	Paignton	1C17	0915CdfPgn	
565	37411		Sa	17	8	1996	Paignton	Cardiff	1B32	1328PgnCdf	
566	37263		Su	18	8	1996	Exeter	Plymouth	1V46	0924LdsPly	+HST
567	37263		Su	18	8	1996	Plymouth	Exeter	1C68	1815PlyBtm	+HST
568	37141		Fr	6	9	1996	Dainton	Exeter	1O03	2215PnzWlo	+47830(DIT)
569	37141		Sa	7	9	1996	Exeter	Plymouth	1C40	1335PadPnz	+HST
570	37141		Fr	13	9	1996	Bristol	Plymouth	1V65	1643YrkPly	+HST
571	37141+37158		Tu	24	9	1996	Exeter	Plymouth	1V57	0910AbdPly	+HST
572	37158		We	25	9	1996	Exeter	Plymouth	1V57	0910AbdPly	+HST
573	37670+37671		Th	3	10	1996	Exeter	Plymouth	1V63	1500NclPly	+37671(M)+HST
574	37670		Mo	7	10	1996	Bridgwater	Exeter	1V48	1217McpPly	+47831(DIT)- term Exeter
575	37521		Tu	8	10	1996	Exeter	Plymouth	1V63	1500NclPly	+HST

Log	_oco	†	dy	date		from	to	code	train	notes
576	37674		Th	17	10 1996	Exeter	Plymouth	1V56	1203NclPly	+HST
577	37895		Th	14	11 1996	Dainton	Bristol	1S71	0722PnzEdb	+HST
578	37673		We	11	12 1996	Par	Penzance	1V29	2350WloPnz	+47832(DIT)
579	37230		Su	15	12 1996	Exeter	Plymouth	1C72	1835PadPnz	+47832(DIT)
580	37254		We	1	1 1997	Exeter	Bristol	1M56	1044PlyMcp	+47829(T)
581	37254		Mo	7	1 1997	Exeter	Bristol	1O03	2215PnzWlo	+47811(DIT)
582	37254		We	15	1 1997	Exeter	Plymouth	1C82	2035PadPly	+HST
583	37229		Fr	21	2 1997	Torquay	Bristol East Yard	1E31	0826PgrNcl	+HST
584	37230		Th	27	2 1997	Plymouth	Bristol	1E40	1650PlySfd	
585	37395		Mo	7	4 1997	Exeter	Penzance	1V29	2350WloPnz	+477xx(T)
586	37412		Sa	24	5 1997	Cardiff	Paignton	1C21	0915CdfPgn	vice sprinter
587	37412		Sa	24	5 1997	Paignton	Cardiff	1B32	1330PgnCdf	vice sprinter
588	37894		We	9	7 1997	Exeter	Plymouth	1C82	2035PadPly	+HST
589	37229		Fr	15	8 1997	Plymouth	Taunton	1M40	1140PlyLvp	Failed at Tnt. 37895 to Bns
590	37275		Th	4	9 1997	Plymouth	Newton Abbot	1M40	1140PlyLvp	Failed at N.Abbot. Term.
591	37887		Mo	29	9 1997	Exeter	Plymouth	1C20	0935PadPly	+HST
592	37521		Tu	14	10 1997	Exeter	Plymouth	1V56	1203NclPly	+HST
593	37230		Su	2	11 1997	Exeter	Plymouth	1V52	1005NclPly	+HST
594	37230		Tu	11	11 1997	Exeter	Birmingham	1M56	1040PlyMcp	+47831(DIT)
595	37673		Su	16	11 1997	Lostwithiel	Plymouth	1S91	1053PnzEdb	+HST then ecs to Exeter
596	37673+37671		Sa	22	11 1997	Plymouth	Bristol	1S35	0922PnzEdb	+HST
597	37263		Mo	24	11 1997	Truro	Penzance	1V29	2350WloPnz	+47813(DIT)
598	37673		Mo	1	12 1997	Exeter	Plymouth	1V63	1502NclPly	+HST
599	37673		We	3	12 1997	Plymouth	Exeter	1S35	0922PnzEdb	+HST
600	37275		Sa	13	12 1997	Exeter	Newton Abbot	1C50	1535PadPnz	+HST
601	37225		Tu	16	12 1997	Exeter	Plymouth	1V35	0604DbyPly	+47839(T)
602	37225		Tu	16	12 1997	Plymouth	Exeter	1M40	1140PlyLvp	+47839(T)
603	37275		We	17	12 1997	Bridgwater	Plymouth	1V63	1502NclPly	+HST. 3o1 late Plymouth
604	37197		Mo	23	3 1998	Yeovil Pen Mill	Exeter	1V29	2350WloPnz	+47811(T)
605	37897+37197		Fr	27	3 1998	Starcross	Newton Abbot	1V57	0910AbdPly	+HST(propelling)
606	37197		Sa	4	4 1998	Exeter	Penzance	1V29	2350WloPnz	+47813(T)+47816(DIT)
607	37197		Th	23	4 1998	Teignmouth	Bristol	1E31	0826PgnNcl	+HST

Log	Loco	†	dy		date		from	to	code	train	notes
608	37674		Sa	2	5	1998	Par	Penzance	1V29	2350WloPnz	+478xx(T)
609	37051		We	3	6	1998	Exeter	Birmingham	1M31	1555PlymMcp	+47701(DIT)
610	37668		Fr	5	6	1998	Truro	Plymouth	1OO3	2200PnzWlo	+47811(DIT)
611	37701		Sa	6	6	1998	Plymouth	Bristol	1M56	0840PnzMcp	+47840(DIT)
612	37701		Sa	6	6	1998	Worle Junction	Exeter	1V46	1017McpPnz	+47807+47791(DIT)
613	37701		Su	7	6	1998	Exeter	Plymouth	1V42	0747McpPly	+HST
614	37025		Su	7	6	1998	Exeter	Plymouth	1V60	1015EdbPnz	+HST
615	37701		Su	7	6	1998	Exeter	Plymouth	1V68	1425NclPly	+HST
616	37025		Tu	9	6	1998	Exeter	Plymouth	1V52	1110GgcPnz	+HST
617	37025		Tu	9	6	1998	Exeter	Plymouth	1V61	1502NclPly	+HST
618	37025		Sa	13	6	1998	Exeter	Newquay	1V49	0814EdbNqy	+HST
619	37701		Sa	13	6	1998	Paignton	Exeter	1M39	1844PgnBns	+47844(DIT)
620	37025		Fr	19	6	1998	Exeter	Plymouth	1V65	1550NclPly	+HST
621	37025		Mo	29	6	1998	Exeter	Plymouth	1V65	1550NclPly	+HST
622	37672		We	1	7	1998	Exeter	Plymouth	1V35	0636WptPly	+47848(DIT)
623	37672		We	1	7	1998	Plymouth	Exeter	1V65	1140PlyMcp	+47848(T)
624	37025		Mo	6	7	1998	Exeter	Penzance	1V50	0639DdePnz	+HST
625	37679		Su	19	7	1998	Exeter	Plymouth	1C82	2015PadPly	+HST
626	37503		Sa	25	7	1998	Newton Abbot	Plymouth	1V29	2350WloPnz	+47846(DIT). Term Plym'th
627	37696		Fr	31	7	1998	Exeter	Plymouth	1V61	1502NclPly	+HST
628	37679+37897		Fr	14	8	1998	Exeter	Penzance	1V50	0840GgcPnz	47831 traction motor fire
629	37897+37679		Fr	15	8	1998	Penzance	Bristol	1M56	0840PnzMcp	37897 to Exeter only
630	37679+37897		Su	23	8	1998	Exeter	Plymouth	1V42	0747McpPly	+HST
631	37679		Sa	29	8	1998	Exeter	Birmingham	1M39	1844PgnBns	+47848(T)
632	37679		Tu	1	9	1998	Exeter	Plymouth	1V61	1502NclPly	+HST
633	37897		Fr	10	9	1998	Exeter	Plymouth	1V61	1502NclPly	+HST
634	37885		Su	13	9	1998	Exeter	Plymouth	1V80	1550NclPly	+HST
635	37513		Th	15	10	1998	Exeter	Bristol	1E36	1300PlyNcl	+HST
636	37040		Th	5	11	1998	Exeter	Plymouth	1C08	0630PadPly	+HST
637	37040		Th	5	11	1998	Plymouth	Exeter	1A52	1100PlyPad	+HST
638	37040		Tu	10	11	1998	Totnes	Plymouth	1V65	1550NclPly	+HST
639	37891		Fr	13	11	1998	Paignton	Exeter	1E31	0821PgnNcl	+HST

Log	Loco	†	dy		date		from	to	code	train	notes
640	37891		Su	22	11	1998	Exeter	Plymouth	1V68	1357NclPly	+HST
641	37047		Mo	28	12	1998	Exeter	Plymouth	1V49	0639DdePnz	+HST. Term Plymouth
642	37047		Su	3	1	1999	Exeter	Plymouth	1V60	1020EdbPnz	+HST
643	37219		Tu	19	1	1999	Exeter	Bristol	1M40	1140PlyLvp	+47831(T)
644	37669		Tu	2	2	1999	Redruth	Penzance	1V50	0840GgcPnz	+47702(DIT)
645	37229		Tu	6	4	1999	Exeter	Plymouth	1V38	0605LdsPly	+HST
646	37229		Tu	6	4	1999	Plymouth	Exeter	1E36	1300PlyLds	+HST
647	37698		Su	11	4	1999	Torquay	Exeter	1A72	1610PgnPad	+HST
648	37042		Fr	7	5	1999	Truro	Plymouth	1M56	0848PnzMcp	+47810(DIT)
649	37692+37351		Fr	7	5	1999	Plymouth	Bristol	1M56	0848PnzMcp	+47810(DIT)
650	37670		Mo	10	5	1999	Par	Penzance	1C00	2350PadPnz	+47846(DIT)
651	37693		Fr	14	5	1999	Exeter	Penzance	1V50	0840GgcPnz	+47840(T)
652	37240+37298		Fr	4	6	1999	St Austell	Penzance	1C42	1432PadPnz	+47832(DIT)
653	37350		Sa	12	6	1999	Bristol	Paignton	1V26	2330McpPgn	+47851(DAR)
654	37350		Sa	12	6	1999	Paignton	Bristol	1S66	0858PgrGgc	+47851(T)
655	37065		Su	18	7	1999	Whiteball	Exeter	1V52	0921NclPly	+HST
656	37695		Sa	7	8	1999	Crewe	Paignton	1V41	0810LvpPgn	+47851(DAR)
657	37695		Sa	7	8	1999	Paignton	Birmingham	1M25	1617PgnMcp	+47851(T)
658	37264		Th	12	8	1999	Plymouth	Bristol	1S35	0922PnzEdb	+HST
659	37174		Th	12	8	1999	Exeter	Plymouth	1V61	1502NclPly	+HST
660	37174		Sa	14	8	1999	Exeter	Paignton	1C05	0700BtmPgn	+47828(DIT)
661	37174		Sa	14	8	1999	Paignton	Bristol	1E33	1001PgnNcl	+47828(DIT)
662	37706		Sa	28	8	1999	Tiverton Jn	Bristol	1E33	1001PgnNcl	+478??(DIT)
663	37694		Sa	1	12	1999	Chacewater	Truro	1A91	1530PadPnz	+HST
664	37670		Sa	14	9	2002	Exeter	Plymouth	1C65	1733PadPly	+HST
665	37425		Sa	4	9	2004	Plymouth	Birmingham	1M25	1420NqyMcp	+HST

Chapter 6 – Class 37 Hauled Rail Tours

The first recorded class 37 hauled rail tour into the South West appears to have occurred on the 31st July 1977 when South Wales based class 37s, 37297 and 37269 double headed the RPPR rail tour from Paddington to Paignton. Heading back in the late afternoon sunshine on a fine summer's day they made an impressive sight.

Many railtours are run to offer the enthusiast a chance to ride behind locomotives that are unusual on passenger trains along a rare stretch of track such as a freight only line, or in a part of the world where that class rarely works passenger services.

Cornwall did not see a class 37 hauled railtour train until the 14th April 1979 when F&W took a pair of 37s to Penzance, along with a single locomotive for a trip to Newquay and back. This was believed to be the first example of a split headcode Class 37, in this case 37084, to work into the county. It travelled west with 37178 and was also a first for a class 37 railtour to Newquay with 37279 making the out and back journey from Par. Trains could still run a round at Newquay in those days right up until the location was rationalized.

Since 1979 Class 37s have continued to visit Devon and Cornwall on railtours, often traversing the local branch lines, bringing the rare chance to sample a loco hauled service on these routes. Writing this in 2019, it is also now rare to see any sort of loco hauled service on the railways of the West Country apart from the overnight sleeper train that still runs between Paddington and Penzance. Fixed formation units now run all the day time services, loco haulage having been discontinued many years ago with the exception in recent years of a summer dated Penzance to Exeter and return outing for a class 57 with the passenger coaching stock off the overnight sleeper train.

Here is a resume of the main Class 37 hauled railtours that have visited Devon and Cornwall over the years. It is not complete but shows the variety of tours, destinations and locomotives that have worked over the years from 1977 to the present date.

31st July 1977 Railway Pictorial Publications 1Z37 "Western Reunion" railtour
37269+37297 from Paddington to Paignton returning at 1730 from Paignton. This was run in conjunction with a trip behind D1062 from Paignton to Kingswear.

14th April 1979 F&W Railtours "Pixieland Express"
0600 Worcester to Penzance with 37178 and 37084. A trip from Par to Newquay was also included utilising 37279 from Par to Newquay and back.

The very first Railtour to the South West featuring class 37s is seen on a hot summers evening at Aller Junction , Newton Abbot . 37269 and 37297 heading the return 1730 Paignton to Paddington Railway Pictorial Publications "Western Reunion " charter – *Photo B. Mills*

37084 is seen at Teingrace on the Heathfield branch. This was the F&W Railtours "The Pixielated Pixie" which ran on the 17th August 1980 and brought an Eastern Region allocated split headcode loco to Devon and Cornwall – *Photo M. Rowe*

26th April 1980 Railway Pictorial Publications railtour "The Penzance Pullman".

37299 with 25155 worked from Plymouth to St Dennis Junction then they returned to Par before continuing onward to Penzance. The return to Plymouth was also handled by this Class 25+37 combination before handing over to 50028.

17th August 1980 F&W Railtours "The Pixielated Pixie" from Cheltenham to Heathfield and Boscarne Junction. 37084 Cheltenham to Bodmin Road via Heathfield. 37142 Bodmin Road to Boscarne Junction then returned the train to Cheltenham.

5th February 1983 B.C.Railtours "The Cornish Crusader" ran from Sheffield to

Plymouth Friary and Newquay. Two class 31s (31235+31327) were in charge between Sheffield and Bristol, giving way there to 37176+37189. 37182 & 37207 took over at Friary for the Cornwall leg of the tour.

6th May 1983 Pathfinder Tours "Skirl O' the Pipes II" from Plymouth to Wick and Thurso departed as 1Z38 1755 from Plymouth behind 37176 and 31187. This combination worked as far as Bristol.

8th May 1983 Pathfinder Tours "Skirl O' the Pipes II" from Plymouth to Wick and Thurso arrived back at Plymouth near midnight on 8th May behind 37187 and 31187.

19th November 1983 B.R. Cornish Branch Lines Railtour

This BR organised tour ran as 1Z10 0815 departure from Bristol Temple Meads powered by two steam heat 37s, 37186 of Cardiff Canton and 37187 of Bristol Bath Road.

The tour visited Carne Point, Parkandillack, Bodmin General and Boscarne Junction before returning to Bristol. Top 'n' tail formation was used on the branch lines.

A scruffy 37186 is seen by the River Fowey near Carne Point 19th November 1983 with the B.R. Cornish Branch Lines Railtour which ran from Bristol Temple Meads – Photo S. C. Marshall

Another view of this tour at Parkandillack 37186 with 37187 in top n tail mode. This view has been transformed in recent years with an incinerator built on the site of the field to the left of the picture – *Photo S. C. Marshall*

3rd March 1984 Hertfordshire Rail tours "Goonbarrow Belle" from London Paddington. 37182+37185 worked the Cornish section from Plymouth which included the Fowey, Parkandillack and Bere Alston branch lines top 'n' tailed.

37182 crossing the River Tavy on the Tavy viaduct which was the former double track main line on the Plymouth to Exeter LSWR route. Now single track it survives as part of the Gunislake branch. This excursion was Hertfordshire Railtours "Goonbarrow Belle" which ran on the 3rd March 1984 – *Photo B. Mills*

The same tour is seen crossing from Cornwall into Devon over the Royal Albert Bridge on 3rd March 1984. 37182 on the front with 37185 on the rear. The tour returned to London Paddington – *Photo B. Mills*

7th April 1984 BR excursion Wolverhampton to Penzance. From Penzance 37207 and 37185 were employed top 'n' tail and made a visit to the Fowey and Parkandillack branch lines.

8th July 1984 F&W Railtours 'The Devonshire Dart' ran from Bristol and Birmingham to Bere Alston, Plymouth Friary and Meldon Quarry. 37185 and 37207 were used between Plymouth and Bere Alston.

26th January 1985 RESL "The Cornishman" tour from London St Pancras to Truro utilized no less than 11 locomotives from classes 20, 25, 31, 37 & 40. The train didn't traverse the Falmouth branch due to late running. 37189+37088 were in charge from Bristol to Plymouth and the return from Plymouth to Bristol via Heathfield. 37207 and 37099 top 'n' tailed to Truro, Parkandillack , Fowey and Plymouth Friary.

7th April 1985 SLOA "The Great Western Limited" steam special from London Paddington to Plymouth as part of The GWR 150 celebrations. Due to the failure of steam locos 6000 and 7819, 37178 and 37007 worked from Exeter to Plymouth.

8th June 1986 FW / Pathfinder "Chopper Topper" railtour from Wolverhampton.
37207 worked the Truro to Falmouth and return to Plymouth section. 37196 derailed at Truro so the train did not travel to Penzance as booked.

Passing Plymouth Laira are 37189 and 37088 with the RESL Cornishman excursion. The tour is returning from Plymouth Friary to London St Pancras via the Heathfield branch. 26th January 1985 – *Photo B. Mills*

Due to the failure of steam locos on the GWR150 special to Plymouth 37007 and 37178 were used to work the service from Exeter to Plymouth on a wet 7th April 1985, seen here departing Newton Abbot. This was unusual as 37178 was actually based at Glasgow Eastfield and 37007 at Gateshead at this time – *Photo S. C. Marshall*

31st August 1986 "Chopper Topper" re-run.

37235 Par to Parkandillack with 37251 top 'n' tail. 37235 Par to Penzance. Two pairs of Class 20s were also involved.

37235 takes the FW Chopper Topper re-run railtour through St Austell station en –route to Penzance. Some now classic cars can be seen in the car park – *Photo R. Geach*

7th June 1987 Branch Line Society "The Meldon Quarryman".

1Z37 Birmingham to Meldon Quarry and Barnstaple utilizing 56081 to Westbury, 47901 to Exeter St Davids, then 37698 from Exeter St Davids to Meldon Quarry and Barnstaple via Crediton before returning to Exeter St Davids.

14th June 1987 Hertfordshire's "Devon Belle".

London Paddington to Meldon Quarry and Barnstaple with 47484 operating to Exeter and 37167 taking the train forward to Mid and North Devon.

4th May 1991 Pathfinder tours "Cornish Centurian 2".

Manchester to Penzance and some Cornish Branch lines. 37673 from Par to Bugle only with 50008 and 50015 the rear.

37698 has arrived at Barnstaple Junction with the Branch Line Society's Meldon Quarryman tour 7th June 1987. Participants line up to get their photos – *Photo S. C. Marshall*

15th September 1991 Pathfinders tour "Tamar Tart".

Manchester to Plymouth Laira open day special 37673+37671 worked Newton Abbot to Paignton and return.

15th September 1991 Hertfordshire Rail Tours "The Plym Rose" return leg Laira depot to Exeter St Davids with 37673+37671. 58027+58041 brought the train from Paddington and returned it from Exeter St Davids.

23rd November 1991 Pathfinder tours "Valiant Thunderer" Manchester to Paignton and Newquay. 37142 piloted from Newton Abbot to Plymouth with 50015 and 50008.

21st March 1992 Merlin Railtours "The Cornish Constructor".

37675 top 'n' tail loco for the Falmouth and Newquay branch. Worked back from Newquay to Plymouth with 33050 and 33063 on the rear.

8th November 1992 DC tours "Exe Solent Explorer" from Waterloo to Exmouth.

37901 & 37906 with 33114 returning from Exmouth to Salisbury where 37178+37278 went forward to Waterloo.

37675 at St Dennis Junction on the Newquay branch. This was Merlin Tours "The Cornish Constructor" top n tail with 33050 and 33063 21st March 1992. This tour also went to Falmouth earlier that day – *Photo R. Geach*

14th November 1992 DC tours "Mule and Otter Axeman" from Waterloo.

This Class 20 hauled railtour had 37092 on the rear from Exeter to Okehampton. It then returned the train to Exeter.

19th June 1993 Hertfordshire Railtours "The Paignton Decorator".

The main railtour engines were a pair of Class 58s but 37191 and 37174 were used to top 'n' tail the train from Newton Abbot to Heathfield.

26th September 1993 BR Area Manager Plymouth special.

37413 with 37669 top 'n' tail Plymouth to Bere Alston and return.

3rd April 1994 Pathfinder Tours "Pixie Railtour" from Bristol Temple Meads to Calstock and Sandplace using 37521 & 37668. The tour in fact the never reached Sandplace due to the failure of 37521 at Plymouth after the return from Calstock. The train continued straight back to Bristol behind 37668 with 37521 dead in train.

2nd May 1994 Pathfinder tours "Torbay Exe-Cursioner" York to Paignton for the Exeter 150 Celebrations. 37896+37796+37799 from Gloucester to Paignton.

Rural Devon on the 26th Sept 1993 and a BR Area Manager Plymouth special is seen with 37669 returning from Bere Alston, near Bere Ferrers, 37413 is on the rear – *Photo R. Geach*

2nd May 1994 Hertfordshire Railtours "The Big E".

37896+37796+37799 worked the return from Exeter to Paddington.

23rd October 1994 Pathfinder Tours "The Pixie Returns" 0750 Bristol Temple Meads to Sandplace on the Looe branch and to Bere Alston. 37412 was the main train engine with 37146 added at Exeter to top 'n' tail on the Looe branch.

7th January 1995 Pathfinder Tours "The Teign Dart" from Wolverhampton to Buckfastleigh and Heathfield. 31417 worked the 7 coach train from Wolverhampton to Totnes and 37695 assisted on the branches.

8th May 1995 Pathfinder Tours "The Grockle Grid" from Wolverhampton to Penzance featured Class 47s to Bristol, 56064 forward to Plymouth returning the train from Penzance. The tour included the Fowey and St Ives branches where 37669+37698 top 'n' tailed.

10th June 1995 Hertfordshire Railtours "Tinners & Knockers" from Derby to Carne Point (Fowey) and Parkandillack. Various Class 47s worked the Derby and Plymouth legs with 37521 and 37670 employed in top 'n' tail mode into Cornwall.

30th September 1995 Pathfinder Tours ran a day trip from Cardiff to Kingswear with dutch liveried 37146 out and back

30th March 1996 Pathfinder Tours "Cornish Raider". A short 4 coach rake headed by 37412 operated as the 0815 Cardiff to Newquay and return. 37671 was added to work the train top 'n' tail from Par to Newquay and back to Par.

37671 at Luxulyan on the Newquay branch with a Pathfinders rail tour from Cardiff to Newquay. 37412 is out of sight on the rear 30th March 1996 – *Photo B. Mills*

17th August 1996 Pathfinder Tours "The Crewe-Chester Flyer" from Exeter St Davids to Chester. 37010+37042 and the return.

5th October 1996 Nenta Railtours "The Devon Rambler" from Norwich to Barnstaple. 37254 & 37671 Exeter to Barnstaple top 'n' tail.

30th November 1996. 37668 ran between Newton Abbot and Heathfield as part of the Newton Abbot 150 Celebrations.

31st December 1996 "Newton Abbot 150 Celebrations" Railtour with 37416 to Heathfield.

17th May 1997 AIA / Pathfinder tours from Preston to Penzance. 37674 top 'n' tail on St Ives branch with 31407+31466 from Penzance. Due to 31466 failing on the return at Penzance 37674 returned the train with 31407 to Birmingham New Street. 31466 was detached at Par.

24th May 1997 Okehampton station re-opening special "Ocean Liner Express".
37415 and 37667 did the honours with a special from Exeter St Davids to Okehampton and back.

37667 is seen at Okehampton station with the Ocean Liner Express. This was the station reopening special from Exeter. 24th May 1997 – *Photo B. Mills*

3rd May 1998 Pathfinder tours "The Cornish Gnome" from Cardiff to Falmouth and Looe with green liveried 37403 and 37669 top 'n' tail from Par to Plymouth on the Cornish branch lines.

5th April 1999 Past Time Railtours "The Heathfield Mule" with Standard steam loco 80079. 37412 worked the 2038 train from Heathfield as far as Newton Abbot.

1st May 1999 37402+37420 "The Cheshire Cheese" ran from Preston to Minehead and return.

25th July 1999 saw 37153 work a Rhymney Valley special from Rhymney to Paignton, outward as a 1Z10 0800 Rhymney-Paignton returning as 1Z11 1645 from Paignton.

37403 carrying its original number D6607 has arrived at Falmouth Docks with the Cornish Gnome, a Pathfinder run tour from Cardiff on 3rd May 1998. 37403 had been repainted into Green with half yellow panels – *Photo R. Geach*

The same tour as above as 37403 heads down the Looe Valley near Terras Bridge. 37669 is on the rear. 3rd May 1998 – *Photo R. Geach*

37669 and 37403, partly hidden by undergrowth, have arrived at Looe on 3rd May 1998. Since the ends of steam haulage back in 1962 this was the first loco hauled passenger service to reach Looe – *Photo R. Geach*

11th August 1999 Scottish Railway Preservation Society "The Total Eclipse" from Linlithgow to Penzance with 37405+37410 throughout. This tour started from Linlithgow on the previous day and conveyed passengers to Penzance overnight to view the Total Solar Eclipse. The return left Penzance just before 5pm on Wednesday 11th August arriving back in Scotland on the following day.

18th September 1999 Pathfinder Tours "Parken Ride" from Crewe to Parkandillack and Fowey branches with 37377+33103 from Crewe to Plymouth. 37417 & 37421 top 'n' tailed on Cornish branch lines and return to Plymouth.

27th July 2002 A Daylight Railtour steam special from Alton to Minehead produced 37308 for the returning 1Z30 1645 from Minehead.

24th August 2002 Past Time Rail. Riley Railways owned 37197 operated the 0910 Exeter to Par 'Eden-ex' out and back.

10th August 2003 Past Time "Torbay Express". The steam loco 7802 Bradley Manor was failed at Kingswear and 37402 was sent down light engine from Bristol to return the 1Z31 1555 Kingswear-Bristol (retimed to a 1715 departure because of a late arrival).

4th October 2003 Merlin Railtours "Atlantic Coast Express". A special powered by 34067 Tangmere utilized 37308 on the Okehampton to Exeter St Davids section.

10th May 2004 Pathfinder Railtours "The Ocean Mail 100".
37197 was used on this tour from Bristol to Kingswear and handed over to 3440 City of Truro for the return.

29th May 2006 Past Time Rail "Fowey Pony" with steam 76079.
37411 did the Carne Point to Plymouth return.

30th May 2006 Past Time Rail "The China Clay Pony" with steam 76079.
37411 worked the Parkandillack to Plymouth return.

31st May 2006 Past Time Rail "The South Hams Pony" with steam 76079.
37411 worked from Newton Abbot to Plymouth.

1st June 2006 Past Time Rail "The Tarka Pony" with steam 76079.
37411 worked the return 1Z19 2118 Barnstaple to Exeter with steam loco on the rear.

9th September 2006 Kingfisher Railtours "Eden and Penzance Explorer".
37405 worked throughout with 1Z82 0603 Bournmouth-Penzance and 1Z83 1627 return.

30th September 2006 Kingfisher Railtours "Eden and Penzance Explorer".
Another offering by Kingfisher took 37406 from Clapham Junction with 1Z21 0610 to Penzance and 1Z22 1644 return.

25th March 2007 Past Time Rail.
As part of a Devon and Cornwall Branch week involving steam loco No 45407. 37410 featured top 'n' tail Par to Falmouth Docks, Truro to Penzance and St Ives to Penzance.

26th March 2007 Past Time Rail Devon and Cornwall Branch week with steam loco 45407. 37410 St Blazey to Par Harbour then Newquay to Plymouth.

27th March 2007 Past Time Rail Devon and Cornwall Branch week "The Tamar Belle" with steam loco 45407. 37410 worked Plymouth to Bere Alston in the morning and Bere Alston to Plymouth Friary in the afternoon.

37410 is seen on the rear of a Bere Alston to Plymouth steam special crossing the creek at Tamerton, Plymouth. 27th March 2007 – *Photo R. Geach*

28th March 2007 Past Time Rail Devon and Cornwall Branch week with steam 45407. 37406 Fowey Docks to Plymouth and Parkandillack to Plymouth.

29th March 2007 Past Time Rail Devon and Cornwall Branch week "The South Hams Pony" with steam 45407. 37410+37406 worked from Exeter St Davids to Plymouth.

31st August 2007 Past Time Rail "Dartmouth Arrow" 1Z37 1026 Bristol Temple Meads to Kingswear and return with EWS liveried 37410+37417 throughout.

2nd September 2007 Past Time Rail "Torbay Express".
Owing to the failure at Bristol of 6024 King Edward I, 37410+37417 worked 1Z27 0919 Bristol Temple Meads to Kingswear and return.

21st June 2008 Spitfire Rail tours "The Paignton Pudden".
DRS liveried 37423+37606 worked Crewe to Paignton and return.

16th May 2009 Pathfinder Tours "Cornish Parker" Crewe to Parkandillack and return 37401+37670 throughout, in top 'n' tail formation on the branch.

6th June 2009 Compass Railtours "The Devonian".

37401+37670 1Z31 0539 Preston to Paignton and return.

27th June 2009 Spitfire Railtours "The Kernow Growler".

37194 piloted DRS partner 37087 westwards on 1Z70 0553 Birmingham International to Penzance returning at 1535, giving participants a 2½ hour break at their destination.

26th June 2010 Spitfire Railtours "Kernow Explorer" for Mazey Day with

DRS pair 37259+37218 on 1Z82 0645 from Gloucester to Penzance and return.

18th September 2010 Vintage Trains "The Down Devonian" Solihull to Plymouth with 37685.

19th September 2010 Vintage Trains ran a series of steam specials on the Looe branch using ex-GWR 9466. Top 'n' tailing was required on several stretches using West Coast 37 37685 which worked Plymouth to Liskeard, then 4 trips from Coombe Jn to Looe and 4 trips from Coombe Jn to Liskeard.

26th September 2010 The above tour was repeated a week later.

In September 2010 Vintage Trains ran a series of steam specials on the Looe branch using ex-GWR Pannier tank No 9466. The operation required top and tailing and West Coast Railways class 37 37685 was used for this purpose, seen at Terras Bridge, near Sandplace, on 19 th September – *Photo R. Geach*

27th September 2010 Vintage Trains "The Up Devonian" Plymouth to Solihull with 37685.

25th June 2011 Spitfire Railtours "Kernow Explorer III" using 37229+37409 from Birmingham International to Penzance and return.

9th June 2012 Pathfinder Tours the "3-2-C" railtour from Crewe to Parkandillack and Heathfield with 37606+37609. 66156 was used from Heathfield to Newton Abbot.

23rd June 2012 Spitfire Railtours "Kernow Explorer" for Mazey Day. 37516+37676 with 1Z37 0500 Birmingham International to Penzance and return.

31st August 2012 Pathfinder Tours "Dartmouth Flyer" brought the DRS pairing of 37259 and 37612 from Tame Bridge to Kingswear with the 1Z37, returning at 1915 as 1Z38.

29th August 2014 Pathfinder Tours "Dartmouth Flyer". 37601+37603 throughout from Crewe to Kingswear and return.

37261 stands in the remains of Truro Goods yard gleaming in its coat of retro green paint. This loco was used to take the empty stock of the City of Truro special back from Truro to Plymouth 30th November 2004 – *Photo R. Geach*

Chapter 7 – Class 37 Component Exchange Overhauls at Plymouth Laira

1988 brought the first class 37 to Plymouth Laira for major overhaul. The BRB policy for the larger Level 5 depots to carry out general overhauls on locomotives that were once sent to the main BREL works, combined with the run down and withdrawal of the class 50 locomotives, meant that Laira had spare capacity.

37047 was the first class 37 selected to be overhauled at Laira. It arrived on the 29th September 1988 and left in December 1988. The second arrival was 37215. 1989 was a busy year for Laira and the following locomotives were dealt with: 37294, 37280, 37252, 37213, 37031, 37053, 37188, 37248, 37273, 37263, 37220 and 37142. 37142's stay was almost three months as it did not depart until February 1990 newly painted in plain Railfreight grey with black numerals. All overhauls included a repaint and the appropriate Railfreight sector decals applied

The last 37 to arrive for overhaul was 37293 during February 1990. It departed in March 1990 but was soon back for rectification work, finally leaving Laira in May 1990.

It is known that some of the overhauled 37s were sent to St Blazey and used on the local clay workings to enable any faults to be rectified before they were sent back to the owning sector. For example, 37252 was noted immaculate in its RFD livery working at St Blazey in June 1989. Likewise 37053 was working at Burngullow on the 10th April 1989. 37188 was observed at Respryn with the Burngullow to Irvine tanks.

An unexpected bonus for the cameraman on the morning of Friday 16th June 1989 was the sight of four light engines heading north by the side of the Teign estuary at Teignmouth. Leading the convoy was 37252, having just been released off a major exam at Plymouth Laira depot, and this was towing 37068 together with two class 50s 50003 and 50048 – *Photo S. C. Marshall*

Low tide at Golant and 37668 approaches the harbor with clay for Fowey on the 30th May 1996. The locomotive is painted in Railfreight Grey with Metals sub sector decals – *Photo R. Geach*

Chapter 8 – Complete list of class 37 passenger workings in loco number order

Loco	log	dy	date	from	to	code	train	detail		miles
6790	1	We	16-Apr-69	Exeter	Bristol	1M91	0740PlyLvp	vb	HU	75.5
D6881	1	Th	03-Jun-65	Paddington	Plymouth		.... PadPly	vb	CF	223.3
" "	2	Th	03-Jun-65	Plymouth	Paddington		.... PlyPad	vb	CF	223.3
D6882	1	Th	03-Jun-65	Paddington	Plymouth		.... PadPly	vb	CF	223.3
" "	2	Th	03-Jun-65	Plymouth	Paddington		.... PlyPad	vb	CF	223.3
37010	1	Fr	24-May-91	Exeter	Barnstaple	2B74	1257ExdBpl	xo	CF	38.9
" "	2	Fr	24-May-91	Barnstaple	Exeter Central	2F19	1414BplExd	xo	CF	38.9
" "	3	Fr	24-May-91	Exeter Central	Barnstaple	2B78	1605ExcBpl	xo	CF	39.7
" "	4	Fr	24-May-91	Barnstaple	Exeter	2B83	1746BplExd	xo	CF	38.9
" "	5	Fr	07-Jun-91	Dainton	Plymouth	1V46	0918McpPly	xo	CF	25.9
" "	6	Sa	10-Aug-91	Exeter	Plymouth	2C13	0800ExmPly	xo	CF	52.0
" "	7	Tu	20-Aug-91	Newton Abbot	Plymouth	1C44	1435PadPnz	xo	CF	31.9
" "	8	We	15-Jan-92	Exeter	Waterloo	2O02	1422ExdWlo	xo	CF	172.4
" "	9	Th	16-Apr-92	Exeter	Yeovil Jn	2O04	1738ExdWlo	xo	CF	49.6
" "	10	Th	16-Apr-92	Yeovil Jn	Exeter	1V17	1655WloExd	xo	CF	49.6
" "	11	Tu	21-Apr-92	Exeter	Salisbury	1O31	0611ExdWlo	xo	CF	88.7
" "	12	Tu	21-Apr-92	Salisbury	Exeter	1V11	1100WloExd	xo	CF	88.7
" "	13	Th	30-Apr-92	Exeter	Plymouth	1C12	0745PadPnz	xo	CF	52.0
" "	14	We	20-May-92	Westbury	Exeter	1C36	1235PadPnz	xo	CF	77.6
" "	15	Tu	26-May-92	Exeter	Salisbury	1O41	1622ExdWlo	xo	CF	88.7
" "	16	Tu	26-May-92	Salisbury	Exeter	1V19	1815WloExd	xo	CF	88.7
" "	17	Tu	02-Jun-92	Exeter	Plymouth	1C02	2355PadPnz	xo	CF	52.0
" "	18	Mo	30-Nov-92	Truro	Bristol	1S35	0925PnzEdb	xo	CF	181.1
" "	19	Mo	27-Feb-95	Cogload Jn	Exeter	1V46	0918LvpPly	xo	TO	35.5
37012	1	We	11-Nov-92	Exeter	Plymouth	1C22	0945PadPly	xi	CF	52.0
" "	2	Mo	05-Apr-93	Exeter	Plymouth	1C32	1135PadPly	xi	CF	52.0
" "	3	We	03-Nov-93	Exeter	Plymouth	1C12	0745PadPnz	xi	BR	52.0
" "	4	We	03-Nov-93	Plymouth	Exeter	1A54	0942PnzPad	xi	BR	52.0
" "	5	We	03-Nov-93	Exeter	Plymouth	1C32	1135PadPly	xi	BR	52.0
37013	1	Su	26-Apr-87	York	Exeter	1V05	1445YrkPly	xo	TE	258.8
37024	1	Sa	27-Jul-85	York	Penzance	1V32	1030YrkPnz	xo	TI	428.1
" "	2	Su	28-Jul-85	Exeter	York	1E92	1340FxdYrk	xo	TI	296.5
37025	1	Su	07-Jun-98	Exeter	Plymouth	1V60	1015EdbPnz	xi	EH	52.0
" "	2	Tu	09-Jun-98	Exeter	Plymouth	1V52	1110GgcPnz	xi	EH	52.0
" "	3	Tu	09-Jun-98	Exeter	Plymouth	1V61	1502NclPly	xi	EH	52.0
" "	4	Sa	13-Jun-98	Exeter	Newquay	1V49	0814EdbNqy	xi	EH	107.6

Loco	log	dy	date	from	to	code	train	detail		miles
" "	5	Fr	19-Jun-98	Exeter	Plymouth	1V65	1550NclPly	xi	EH	52.0
" "	6	Mo	29-Jun-98	Exeter	Plymouth	1V65	1550NclPly	xi	EH	52.0
" "	7	Mo	06-Jul-98	Exeter	Penzance	1V50	0639DdePnz	xi	EH	131.6
37031	1	Fr	10-Aug-84	York	Plymouth	1Z49	1420YrkPly	xo	HM	348.6
37035	1	Th	16-May-91	Exeter St.Davids	Exeter Central	1A03	2215PnzPad	xo	CF	0.8
" "	2	Mo	27-May-91	Exeter	Plymouth	1C32	1135PadPly	xi	CF	52.0
" "	3	Mo	27-May-91	Exeter	Plymouth	1C66	1835PadPly	xi	CF	52.0
" "	4	Mo	10-Jun-91	Honiton	Exeter	1V17	1655WloExd	xi	CF	17.4
" "	5	Mo	05-Jul-93	Newton Abbot	Bristol	1M40	1144PlyLvp	xo	CF	95.7
" "	6	Sa	10-Jul-93	Exeter	Bristol		0955PgnMcp	xi	CF	75.5
37038	1	Sa	01-Jun-91	Exeter	Paddington	1A52	1130PgnPad	xo	CF	173.5
" "	2	Mo	13-Apr-92	Exeter	Salisbury	2O02	1422ExdWlo	xo	CF	88.7
" "	3	Mo	13-Apr-92	Salisbury	Exeter	1V17	1655WloExd	xo	CF	88.7
" "	4	Mo	20-Apr-92	Axminster	Exeter	1V19	1855WloExd	xo	CF	27.6
" "	5	Tu	21-Apr-92	Newton Abbot	Exeter	2C08	0712NabExd	xo	CF	20.2
" "	6	Sa	25-Sep-93	Paignton	Bristol	1M42	1611PgnLvp	xo	CF	103.8
" "	7	Fr	12-Nov-93	Exeter	Bristol	1M56	1015PlyMcp	xo	CF	75.5
" "	8	Sa	08-Jan-94	Exeter	Plymouth	1C22	0835PadPly	xo	CF	52.0
" "	9	Sa	08-Jan-94	Plymouth	Exeter	1A61	1335PlyPad	xo	CF	52.0
" "	10	Tu	05-Apr-94	Exeter	Reading	1A54	0942PnzPad	xo	CF	137.8
" "	11	Th	30-Jun-94	Exeter	Bristol	1M40	1144PlyLvp	xo	CF	75.5
37040	1	Tu	09-Nov-93	Exeter	Plymouth	1V48	1018LvpPly	xo	CF	52.0
" "	2	Th	27-Jan-94	Exeter	Plymouth		0935PadPly	xo	CF	52.0
" "	3	Th	05-Nov-98	Exeter	Plymouth	1C08	0630PadPly	xo	EH	52.0
" "	4	Th	05-Nov-98	Plymouth	Exeter	1A52	1100PlyPad	xo	EH	52.0
" "	5	Tu	10-Nov-98	Totnes	Plymouth	1V65	1550NclPly	xo	EH	23.2
" "	6	Fr	04-Jun-99	St Austell	Penzance	1C42	1432PadPnz	xo	TO	40.2
37042	1	Su	13-Jun-93	Totnes	Bristol		0835PlyPad	xo	CF	104.0
" "	2	Fr	07-May-99	Truro	Plymouth	1M56	0848PnzMcp	xo	TO	53.6
37046	1	Mo	26-Apr-93	Exeter	Basingstoke	1O41	1622ExdWlo	xo	CF	124.6
37047	1	Mo	28-Dec-98	Exeter	Plymouth	1V49	0639DdePnz	xo	TO	52.0
" "	2	Su	03-Jan-99	Exeter	Plymouth	1V60	1020EdbPnz	xo	TO	52.0
37050	1	Sa	26-May-79	York	Newton Abbot	1V81	1043YrkNab	xb	MR	309.8
" "	2	Sa	26-May-79	Newton Abbot	York	1E00	2230NabYrk	xb	MR	309.8
37051	1	We	03-Jun-98	Exeter	Birmingham	1M31	1555PlyMcp	xi	TO	165.6
37052	1	Sa	22-Jun-85	Birmingham	Paignton	1V58	2215GgcPgn	xi	MR	193.9
" "	2	Sa	22-Jun-85	Paignton	Birmingham	1M86	1000PgnLvp	xi	MR	193.9
37054	1	We	20-Feb-91	Exeter	Plymouth	1V56	1142NclPnz	xi	CF	52.0
" "	2	Sa	23-Feb-91	Exeter	Bristol	1A03	2215PnzPad	xi	CF	75.5
" "	3	Su	07-Jul-91	Exeter	Plymouth	1C62	1635PadPly	xi	CF	52.0
" "	4	Mo	22-Jun-92	Exeter	Plymouth	1V48	1015LvpPly	xi	CF	52.0
" "	5	Mo	22-Jun-92	Plymouth	Exeter	1E39	1710PlyLds	xi	CF	52.0
" "	6	Sa	27-Jun-92	Exeter	Plymouth	1C02	0005PadPnz	xi	CF	52.0
" "	7	Mo	10-Aug-92	Exeter	Plymouth	1C50	1535PadPnz	xi	CF	52.0
" "	8	Su	30-Aug-92	Exeter	Plymouth	1C17	1017BtmPly	xi	CF	52.0
" "	9	Mo	31-Aug-92	Tiverton Pkwy	Taunton	1E29	0625PlyNcl	xi	CF	13.2
" "	10	Fr	20-Nov-92	Feniton	Exeter	1V15	1515WloExd	xi	CF	52.0
" "	11	Su	06-Dec-92	Exeter	Plymouth	1C72	1835PadPly	xi	CF	52.0

Loco	log	dy	date	from	to	code	train	detail		miles
" "	12	Tu	08-Dec-92	Exeter	Waterloo	1O41	1622ExdWlo	xi	CF	172.4
" "	13	We	09-Dec-92	Exeter	Plymouth	1V59	0900AbdPly	xi	CF	52.0
" "	14	Sa	11-Sep-83	Exeter	Penzance		2300LdsNqy	xi	CF	131.6
" "	15	Sa	18-Sep-93	Exeter	Plymouth	1V47	1018McpPnz	xi	BR	52.0
37058	1	Sa	17-Aug-85	York	Penzance	1V32	1030YrkPnz	xo	GD	428.1
37061	1	Mo	19-Aug-85	York	Penzance	1V32	1030YrkPnz	vo	GD	428.1
" "	2	Fr	30-Aug-85	Plymouth	Leeds	1E50	1100PlyLds	vo	GD	334.6
37064	1	Sa	19-May-79	Norwich	Paignton	1Z ..	0910NrwPgn	xo	SF	357.2
37065	1	Su	18-Jul-99	Whiteball	Exeter	1V52	0921NclPly	xo	TO	23.7
37075	1	Sa	02-Jun-84	Newcastle	Plymouth	1V48	2030NclNqy	xi	HM	421.8
37076	1	Sa	09-Jul-83	Birmingham	Paignton	1V73	0820LvpPgn	xo	TE	193.9
" "	2	Sa	09-Jul-83	Paignton	Wolverhampton	1M54	1505PgnWpt	xo	TE	206.8
37077	1	Sa	25-Sep-93	Dawlish Warren	Plymouth	1V35	0605DbyPnz	xo	BR	41.5
" "	2	Tu	22-Feb-94	Exeter	Plymouth	1C54	1635PadPly	xo	SF	52.0
" "	3	Tu	29-Mar-94	Exeter	Plymouth	1C82	2035PadPly	xo	SF	52.0
37078	1	Tu	11-Feb-86	Bristol	Exeter	1C09	0635BtmPly	xo	TE	76.5
37082	1	Sa	13-Jul-85	Birmingham	Paignton	1V58	2215GgcPgn	vo	GD	195.5
" "	2	Sa	13-Jul-85	Paignton	Birmingham	1M86	1000PgnLvp	vo	GD	193.9
" "	3	Mo	15-Jul-85	Birmingham	Newton Abbot		1020GgcPly	vo	GD	185.8
37083	1	Mo	11-Mar-91	Exeter	Plymouth	1C54	1635PadPly	xo	CF	52.0
" "	2	We	20-Mar-91	Plymouth	Birmingham	1S71	0716PnzAbd	xo	CF	217.7
37092	1	Th	11-Jun-92	Exeter	Bristol	1M48	1548PlyDby	xi	CF	75.5
" "	2	Sa	12-Dec-92	Axminster	Exeter	2V05	0615SalExd	xi	CF	27.6
" "	3	We	23-Dec-92	Exeter	Plymouth	1V56	1205NclPly	xi	CF	52.0
" "	4	Tu	05-Jan-93	Exeter	Reading	1A03	2215PnzPad	xi	CF	157.9
" "	5	Su	20-Jun-93	Paddington	Paignton	1Z60	0840PadPgn	xi	CF	221.3
" "	6	Su	20-Jun-93	Paignton	Paddington	1Z60	1740PgnPad	xi	CF	221.3
37096	1	Th	09-Aug-84	York	Plymouth	1V31	1030YrkPly	xo	TE	348.6
" "	2	Sa	11-Aug-84	Liskeard	Penzance	1V64	0717DbyPnz	xo	TE	61.8
37097	1	Su	07-Jul-91	Totnes	Exeter	1M62	0855PlyMcp	xo	CF	28.9
" "	2	Su	07-Jul-91	Exeter	Plymouth	1V62	1610McpPly	xo	CF	52.0
" "	3	We	04-Mar-92	Exeter	Plymouth	1C02	0005PadPnz	xo	CF	52.0
" "	4	Su	27-Mar-94	Exeter	Plymouth	1C66	1735PadPnz	xo	BR	52.0
37098	1	Mo	04-Mar-91	Exeter	Bristol	1S85	0710PlyEdb	xo	CF	75.5
" "	2	Su	17-Mar-91	Exeter	Plymouth		1555NclPly	xo	CF	52.0
" "	3	Mo	29-Jul-91	Exeter	Plymouth	1V48	1016LvpPly	xo	CF	52.0
" "	4	Mo	29-Jul-91	Plymouth	Exeter	1E39	1710PlyLds	xo	CF	52.0
" "	5	Tu	13-Aug-91	Exeter	Newton Abbot	2C13	0800ExmNab	xo	CF	20.2
" "	6	Mo	19-Aug-91	Exeter	Plymouth	1V52	0944GgcPnz	xo	CF	52.0
" "	7	Sa	24-Aug-91	Exeter	Paignton	1V41	0720NtmPgn	xo	CF	28.3
" "	8	Sa	24-Aug-91	Paignton	Exeter	1M86	1345PgnNtm	xo	CF	28.3
" "	9	Sa	24-Aug-91	Exeter	Newton Abbot	1V49	0752NclPgn	xo	CF	20.2
" "	10	We	28-Aug-91	Exeter	Plymouth	1V56	1205NclPly	xo	CF	52.0
" "	11	Fr	30-Aug-91	Plymouth	Exeter	1A70	1236PnzPad	xo	CF	52.0
" "	12	Sa	28-Sep-91	Exeter	Bristol	1A03	2135PnzPad	xo	CF	75.5
" "	13	Su	29-Sep-91	Exeter	Salisbury	2O03	1722ExdWlo	xo	CF	88.7
" "	14	Su	29-Sep-91	Salisbury	Exeter	1V19	1855WloExd	xo	CF	88.7
" "	15	Th	03-Dec-92	Exeter	Plymouth		0950GgcPnz	xo	CF	52.0

Loco	log	dy	date	from	to	code	train		detail	miles
" "	16	Su	06-Dec-92	Exeter	Salisbury	1O35	0928ExdWlo	xo	CF	88.7
" "	17	Su	06-Dec-92	Salisbury	Exeter	1V11	1055WloExd	xo	CF	88.7
" "	18	Th	25-Mar-93	Honiton?	Exeter	1V15	1515WloExd	xo	CF	17.4
37099	1	Fr	26-Jan-85	Bristol	Exeter	1C09	0635BtmPly	xb	MR	76.5
37101	1	Su	11-Aug-85	Derby	Plymouth	1V40	1055DbyPly	xo	TE	258.9
" "	2	Fr	31-Jan-86	Bristol	Exeter	1C09	0635BtmPly	xo	GD	76.5
37102	1	Mo	07-Jun-82	Torquay	Birmingham	1E12	1115TqyNcl	xb	MR	191.8
37109	1	We	01-Sep-93	Exeter	Plymouth	1C44	1435PadPnz	xi	BR	52.0
37126	1	Sa	01-Sep-79	Derby	Paignton	1V62	0732DbyPgn	xo	IM	235.1
" "	2	Sa	01-Sep-79	Paignton	Derby	1E91	1505PgnLds	xo	IM	235.1
37129	1	Tu	18-Mar-86	Bristol	Exeter	1C09	0635BtmExd	xo	BR	76.5
37131	1	Sa	01-Aug-87	Par	Plymouth	1M45	1133PnzLvp	xo	TI	34.8
37133	1	Fr	01-Nov-91	Exeter	Gloucester	2B18	1540ExdGlr	xo	CF	115.6
" "	2	Su	10-Nov-91	Honiton	Exeter	1V08	0745BskExd	xo	CF	17.4
37135	1	We	23-Jul-86	Bodmin Parkway	Plymouth	1S71	0730PnzAbd	xo	BR	26.9
" "	2	Sa	30-Aug-86	Newton Abbot?	Plymouth	1V64	1200LvpPnz	xo	BR	31.9
37137	1	Tu	17-Jan-95	Exeter	Plymouth	1V38	0605LdsPly	xo		52.0
" "	2	Tu	17-Jan-95	Plymouth	Exeter	1E36	1300PlyLds	xo		52.0
37140	1	Sa	03-Apr-93	Woking	Exeter	2V21	1915WloExd	xo	SF	148.1
37141	1	We	03-Apr-91	Exeter Central	Barnstaple	2B80	1730ExcBpl	xo	CF	39.7
" "	2	We	03-Apr-91	Barnstaple	Exeter	2B85	1925BplExd	xo	CF	38.9
" "	3	We	19-Jun-91	Crewkerne	Exeter	2V13	1315WloExd	xo	CF	49.6
" "	4	Sa	20-Jul-91	Paignton	Exeter	1M78	1216PgnMcp	xo	CF	28.3
" "	5	Tu	23-Jul-91	Exeter	Plymouth	1V48	1016LvpPly	xo	CF	52.0
" "	6	Tu	23-Jul-91	Plymouth	Bristol	1E39	1710PlyLds	xo	CF	127.5
" "	7	Th	28-Nov-91	Exeter	Plymouth	1V48	1016LvpPly	xo	CF	52.0
" "	8	Th	28-May-92	Exeter	Plymouth	1C12	0745PadPnz	xo	CF	52.0
" "	9	Mo	12-Oct-92	Exeter	Plymouth	1V52	0944GgcPnz	xo	CF	52.0
" "	10	Tu	27-Oct-92	Exeter	Salisbury	1O41	1622ExdWlo	xo	CF	88.7
" "	11	Tu	27-Oct-92	Salisbury	Exeter	1V19	1815WloExd	xo	CF	88.7
" "	12	Th	29-Oct-92	Exeter	Salisbury	1O41	1622ExdWlo	xo	CF	88.7
" "	13	Th	29-Oct-92	Salisbury	Exeter	1V19	1815WloExd	xo	CF	88.7
" "	14	Su	01-Nov-92	Exeter	Plymouth	1C56	1535PadPnz	xo	CF	52.0
" "	15	Sa	17-Apr-93	Newton Abbot	Exeter	1S85	0725PlyAbd	xo	CF	20.2
" "	16	Fr	08-Jul-94	Exeter	Bristol	1A24	0640ExdPad	xo	CF	75.5
" "	17	Mo	24-Oct-94	Exeter	Plymouth	1C02	2355PadPnz	xo	CF	52.0
" "	18	Mo	27-Mar-95	Taunton	Exeter	1V35	0643WvpPly	xo	CF	30.8
" "	19	Mo	27-Mar-95	Exeter	Bristol	1M40	1144PlyLvp	xo	CF	75.5
" "	20	Sa	12-Aug-95	Rewe	Exeter	1V46	0605GgcPgn	xo	CF	7.0
" "	21	Fr	06-Sep-96	Dainton	Exeter	1O03	2215PnzPad	xo	CF	24.1
" "	22	Sa	07-Sep-96	Exeter	Plymouth	1C40	1335PadPnz	xo	CF	52.0
" "	23	Fr	13-Sep-96	Bristol	Plymouth	1V63	1043YrkPly	xo	CF	127.5
" "	24	Tu	24-Sep-96	Exeter	Plymouth	1V57	0910AbdPly	xo	CF	52.0
37142	1	Fr	08-Sep-78	St Germans	Penzance	1B02	0005PadPnz	xo	LA	70.0
" "	2	Sa	16-Jun-79	Par	Newquay	2B72	1200ParNqy	xo	LA	20.8
" "	3	Sa	16-Jun-79	Newquay	Par	1M31	1402NqyBns	xo	LA	20.8
" "	4	Fr	27-Jun-80	Bodmin Road	Plymouth		0620PnzPly	xo	LA	26.9
" "	5	Sa	23-Aug-80	Newquay	Plymouth	1E22	0950NqyNcl	xo	LA	55.5

Loco	log	dy	date	from	to	code	train	detail		miles
" "	6	Sa	30-May-81	Plymouth	Penzance	2B36	1745PlyPnz	xo	LA	79.5
" "	7	Sa	13-Jun-81	Penzance	Plymouth	1M83	1050PnzMcp	xo	LA	44.7
" "	8	Sa	01-Aug-81	Par	Plymouth	1A09	1035NqyPad	xo	LA	34.8
" "	9	Mo	21-Dec-87	Exeter	Plymouth		0657NclPly	xo	LA	52.0
" "	10	Mo	21-Dec-87	Plymouth	Bristol		1450PlyYrk	xo	LA	127.5
" "	11	Tu	26-Jan-88	Exeter	Paignton	2C20	1745ExmPgn	xo	CF	28.3
" "	12	Tu	26-Jan-88	Paignton	Exeter	2C51	1917PgnExd	xo	CF	28.3
" "	13	Sa	23-Nov-91	Plymouth	Paddington	1A61	1335PlyPad	xo	CF	225.5
" "	14	Th	28-Nov-91	Honiton	Exeter	1V11	1115WloExd	xo	CF	17.4
" "	15	Sa	13-Aug-94	Exeter	Reading	1A16	0643ExdRdg	xo	CF	137.5
" "	16	Tu	03-Jan-95	Exeter	Bristol	1M48	1545PlyDby	xo	CF	75.5
37146	1	Tu	22-Jan-91	Exeter	Barnstaple	2B76	1515ExdBpl	xo	CF	38.9
" "	2	Tu	22-Jan-91	Barnstaple	Exeter	2B77	1618BplExd	xo	CF	38.9
" "	3	We	23-Jan-91	Exeter Central	Barnstaple	2B78	1605ExcBpl	xo	CF	39.7
" "	4	We	23-Jan-91	Barnstaple	Exeter	2B83	1746BplExd	xo	CF	39.7
" "	5	Fr	25-Jan-91	Exeter	Barnstaple	2B76	1515ExdBpl	xo	CF	38.9
" "	6	Fr	25-Jan-91	Barnstaple	Exeter	2B77	1618BplExd	xo	CF	38.9
" "	7	Fr	25-Jan-91	Exeter	Barnstaple	2B80	1736ExdBpl	xo	CF	38.9
" "	8	Fr	25-Jan-91	Barnstaple	Exeter	2B85	1925BplExd	xo	CF	38.9
" "	9	Mo	20-May-91	Westbury	Exeter	1C66	1835PadPly	xo	CF	77.9
" "	10	Tu	02-Mar-93	Exeter	Salisbury	1O35	0945ExdWlo	xo	CF	88.7
" "	11	Tu	02-Mar-93	Salisbury	Exeter	1V11	1115WloExd	xo	CF	88.7
" "	12	Mo	22-Mar-93	Exeter	Salisbury	1O41	1622ExdWlo	xo	CF	88.7
" "	13	Mo	22-Mar-93	Salisbury	Exeter	1V19	1815WloExd	xo	CF	88.7
" "	14	Sa	11-Jun-94	Exeter	Plymouth	1C76	1930PadPly	xo	CF	52.0
" "	15	Fr	03-Mar-95	Exeter	Plymouth	1V63	1500NclPly	xo	CF	52.0
" "	16	Th	16-Mar-95	Dainton	Bristol	1E48	1545PlySfd	xo	CF	99.6
37158	1	Fr	22-Nov-85	Bristol	Exeter	1C09	0635BtmPly	xo	BR	76.5
" "	2	Tu	25-Mar-86	Bristol	Exeter	1C09	0635BtmPly	xo	BR	76.5
" "	3	Su	09-Dec-90	Exeter	Plymouth	1C44	1235PadPnz	xo	CF	52.0
" "	4	Mo	24-Dec-90	Exeter	Honiton	2B81	1707PlmHon	xo	CF	17.4
" "	5	Mo	24-Dec-90	Honiton	Exeter	2B84	1905HonExd	xo	CF	17.4
" "	6	Mo	07-Jan-91	Paignton	Exeter		1444PgnExd	xo	CF	28.3
" "	7	Mo	23-Sep-91	Exeter	Plymouth	1V35	0605DbyPly	xo	CF	52.0
" "	8	Mo	23-Sep-91	Plymouth	Exeter	1M56	1203PlyMcp	xo	CF	52.0
" "	9	Th	26-Sep-91	Dawlish	Plymouth	1C28	1035PadPnz	xo	CF	39.9
" "	10	Su	20-Jun-93	Paddington	Paignton	1Z60	0840PadPgn	xo	CF	221.3
" "	11	Su	20-Jun-93	Paignton	Paddington	1Z60	1740PgnPad	xo	CF	221.3
" "	12	Tu	25-Oct-94	Exeter	Penzance		1735PadPnz	xo	CF	131.6
" "	13	Th	02-Feb-95	Plymouth	Bristol	1S19	2045PlyGgc	xo	CF	127.5
" "	14	Su	22-Apr-95	Paignton	Exeter		1500PgnPad	xo	CF	28.3
" "	15	Mo	12-Jun-95	Exeter	Plymouth	1C28	1035PadPnz	xo	CF	52.0
" "	16	Fr	16-Jun-95	Exeter	Plymouth	1V35	0604DbyPly	xo	CF	52.0
" "	17	Fr	16-Jun-95	Plymouth	Bristol	1M40	1144PlyLvp	xo	CF	127.5
" "	18	Fr	16-Jun-95	Bristol	Exeter	1V49	0943YrkExd	xo	CF	75.5
" "	19	Fr	23-Jun-95	Exeter	Plymouth	1C50	1535PadPnz	xo	CF	52.0
" "	20	Sa	24-Jun-95	Exeter	Plymouth	1V30	2004EdbPnz	xo	CF	52.0
" "	21	Th	31-Aug-95	Exeter	Plymouth	1C66	1835PadPly	xo	CF	52.0

Loco	log	dy	date	from	to	code	train		detail	miles
" "	22	Fr	01-Sep-95	Exeter	Plymouth	1C28	1035PadPnz	xo	CF	52.0
" "	23	We	18-Oct-95	Exeter	Plymouth	1C54	1635PadPly	xo	CF	52.0
" "	24	Fr	20-Oct-95	Exeter	Plymouth	1C32	1135PadPly	xo	CF	52.0
" "	25	Fr	26-Jan-96	Exeter	Plymouth	1C82	2035PadPly	xo	CF	52.0
" "	26	Su	17-Mar-96	Exeter	Plymouth	1C66	1310EdbPnz	xo	CF	52.0
" "	27	Fr	12-Apr-96	Exeter	Plymouth	1C44	1445PadPnz	xo	CF	52.0
" "	28	Tu	24-Sep-96	Exeter	Plymouth	1V57	0910AbdPly	xo	CF	52.0
" "	29	We	25-Sep-96	Exeter	Plymouth	1V57	0910AbdPly	xo	CF	52.0
37165	1	Sa	24-Aug-85	Birmingham	Paignton	1V58	2215GgcPgn	xo	CF	193.9
" "	2	Sa	24-Aug-85	Paignton	Birmingham	1M86	1000PgnLvp	xo	CF	193.9
37169	1	Sa	05-Jun-76	Bristol	Paignton	1V69	0925BnsPgn	xo	TI	103.8
" "	2	Sa	05-Jun-76	Paignton	Bristol	1M60	1500PgnMcp	xo	II	103.8
371/4	1	We	01-May-91	Exeter	Yeovil Jn	2O04	1737ExdWlo	xo	CF	49.7
" "	2	Sa	29-May-93	Paignton	Exeter	1S93	1518PgnGgc	xo	CF	28.3
" "	3	Sa	29-May-93	Exeter	Plymouth	1C54	1635PadPly	xo	CF	52.0
" "	4	Fr	11-Jun-93	Crewkerne	Exeter	1V17	1730WloExd	xo	CF	40.7
" "	5	Tu	29-Jun-93	Exeter	Plymouth	1C22	0945PadPly	xo	CF	52.0
" "	6	We	11-Aug-93	Westbury	Plymouth	1C32	1135PadPly	xo	BR	129.9
" "	7	We	11-Aug-93	Exeter	Plymouth	1V59	0900AbdPly	xo	BR	52.0
" "	8	Fr	11-Feb-94	Exeter	Plymouth	1V56	1205NclPly	xo	TO	52.0
" "	9	Su	13-Feb-94	Exeter	Bristol	1S19	2100PlyGgc	xo	CF	75.5
" "	10	Th	12-Aug-99	Exeter	Plymouth	1V61	1502NclPly	xo	TO	52.0
" "	11	Sa	14-Aug-99	Exeter	Paignton	1C05	0700BtmPgn	xo	TO	28.3
" "	12	Sa	14-Aug-99	Paignton	Bristol	1E33	1001PgnNcl	xo	TO	103.8
37175	1	We	26-Nov-86	Lostwithiel	Plymouth	1A50	1000PnzPad	xi	LA	30.3
" "	2	Th	03-Sep-87	Exeter	Barnstaple	1C07	0405ExdBpl	xi	LA	38.9
" "	3	Th	03-Sep-87	Barnstaple	Exeter	2C68	0545BplPnz	xi	LA	38.9
" "	4	Fr	04-Sep-87	Exeter	Barnstaple	1C07	0405ExdBpl	xi	LA	38.9
" "	5	Fr	04-Sep-87	Barnstaple	Exeter	2C68	0545BplPnz	xi	LA	38.9
" "	6	Sa	05-Sep-87	Kings Nympton	Exeter	2B75	1352BplExd	xi	LA	25.3
37177	1	Sa	22-Sep-84	Birmingham	Paignton	1V71	0820LvpPgn	xb	LE	193.9
" "	2	Sa	22-Sep-84	Paignton	Birmingham	1M65	1608PgnLvp	xb	LE	193.9
37178	1	Th	01-Jun-95	Exeter	Plymouth	1V48	1217McpPly	xi	CF	52.0
" "	2	Tu	06-Jun-95	Plymouth	Penzance	1C50	1535PadPnz	xi	CF	79.5
" "	3	Su	11-Jun-95	Exeter	Penzance	1C20	0910PadPnz	xi	CF	131.6
" "	4	Su	11-Jun-95	Penzance	Exeter	1A92	1540PnzPad	xi	CF	131.6
37181	1	Sa	28-May-83	Tremake	Penzance	1Z50	1147PadPnz	xb	LA	44.0
" "	2	Mo	29-Aug-83	Lostwithiel	Penzance	1V76	0920LvpPnz	xi	LA	49.2
" "	3	Su	15-Apr-84	Par	Plymouth	1A07	2135PnzPad	xb	LA	34.8
" "	4	Sa	09-Jun-84	Penzance	Plymouth	1Z26	0545PnzWem	xo	LE	79.5
" "	5	Fr	27-Jul-84	Paignton	Bristol	1S81	1928PgnGgc	xi	LA	103.8
" "	6	Sa	25-Aug-84	Plymouth	Exeter	1A79	1448PnzPad	xi	LA	52.0
" "	7	Fr	12-Apr-85	Bodmin Parkway	Lostwithiel	1V76	0936LvpPnz	xi	LA	4.0
" "	8	Su	31-Aug-86	Truro	Falmouth		....TruFal	xb	LA	11.8
" "	9	Su	31-Aug-86	Falmouth	Truro		....FalTru	xb	LA	11.8
" "	10	Su	31-Aug-86	Truro	Falmouth		....TruFal	xb	LA	11.8
" "	11	Su	31-Aug-86	Falmouth	Truro		....FalTru	xb	LA	11.8
37182	1	Su	30-Jan-83	Exeter	Plymouth		1230EdbPly	xb	LA	52.0

Loco	log	dy	date	from	to	code	train	detail		miles
" "	2	Fr	17-May-85	Bristol	Exeter	1C09	0635BtmPly	xi	BR	76.5
37183	1	Tu	15-Jan-80	Cardiff	Plymouth	1B26	0756CdfPly	xb	LE	165.7
" "	2	Tu	15-Jan-80	Plymouth	Cardiff	1C60	1330PlySwa	xb	LE	165.7
37185	1	Sa	08-Sep-84	Par	Penzance		0917ParPnz	xi	LA	44.8
" "	2	Tu	29-Oct-85	Bristol	Exeter	1C09	0635BtmPly	xo	BR	76.5
" "	3	Fr	21-Oct-88	Exeter	Plymouth	1V50	0850GgcPnz	xo	TI	52.0
37191	1	Fr	09-Nov-90	Exeter	Salisbury	1Z40	1505ExdSal	xi	CF	88.7
" "	2	Tu	10-Sep-91	Exeter	Plymouth	1C12	0745PadPnz	xi	CF	52.0
" "	3	Su	27-Jun-93	Newton Abbot	Exeter		1242PnzPad	xi	CF	20.2
" "	4	Fr	02-Jul-93	Exeter	Plymouth	1V49	0945YrkPly	xi	CF	52.0
" "	5	Tu	17-May-94	Exeter	Bristol	1S19	2045PlyGgc	xi	CF	75.5
" "	6	Fr	03-Jun-94	Exeter	Plymouth	1C54	1635PadPly	xi	CF	52.0
" "	7	Th	01-Sep-94	Rewe	Exeter		0835BtmPly	xi	CF	7.0
37196	1	Fr	12-Apr-85	Lostwithiel	Penzance	1V76	0936LvpPnz	xo	LA	49.2
" "	2	Tu	30-Jul-85	Par	Plymouth	1A73	1346PnzPad	xo	LA	34.8
" "	3	Sa	22-Feb-86	Par	Penzance	1V76	0936LvpPnz	xo	LA	49.2
" "	4	Th	13-Mar-86	Penzance	Plymouth	2C86	1527PnzPly	xo	LA	79.5
37197	1	Sa	18-May-85	Birmingham	Paignton	1V71	0820LvpPgn	xo	CF	193.9
" "	2	Tu	27-Oct-92	Plymouth	Exeter		0646PnzPad	xo	CF	52.0
" "	3	Su	10-Jan-93	Exeter	Plymouth	1C56	1535PadPnz	xo	CF	52.0
" "	4	Su	10-Jan-93	Exeter	Plymouth	1V58	1125EdbPnz	xo	CF	52.0
" "	5	Su	07-Feb-93	Exeter	Plymouth	1C53	1508RdgPnz	xo	CF	52.0
" "	6	We	17-Feb-93	Exeter	Plymouth	1C60	1735PadPnz	xo	CF	52.0
" "	7	Th	04-Mar-93	Gillingham	Exeter	1V11	1115WloExd	xo	CF	67.0
" "	8	Su	20-Jun-93	Paddington	Paignton	1Z60	0840PadPgn	xo	CF	221.3
" "	9	Su	20-Jun-93	Paignton	Paddington	1Z60	1740PgnPad	xo	CF	221.3
" "	10	Th	15-Sep-94	Exeter	Plymouth		0640DdePnz	xo	CF	52.0
" "	11	Th	06-Oct-94	Exeter	Plymouth		0640DdePnz	xo	CF	52.0
" "	12	Tu	13-Jun-95	Taunton	Plymouth	1C32	1135PadPly	xo	CF	82.8
" "	13	Th	20-Jul-95	Exeter	Penzance	1C12	0745PadPnz	xo	CF	131.6
" "	14	Th	20-Jul-95	Penzance	Exeter	1A81	1440PnzPad	xo	CF	131.6
" "	15	Fr	04-Aug-95	Exeter	Plymouth	1C22	0945PadPly	xo	CF	52.0
" "	16	Fr	11-Aug-95	Exeter	Reading	1A76	1535PlyPad	xo	CF	137.5
" "	17	Fr	18-Aug-95	Teignmouth	Plymouth	1V35	0604DbyPly	xo	CF	37.1
" "	18	Fr	18-Aug-95	Plymouth	Bristol	1M40	1144PlyLvp	xo	CF	127.5
" "	19	Fr	18-Aug-95	Exeter	Plymouth	1C54	1635PadPly	xo	CF	52.0
" "	20	We	20-Sep-95	Exeter	Plymouth	1C22	0935PadPly	xo	CF	52.0
" "	21	We	12-Jun-96	Exeter	Plymouth	1C28	1045PadPnz	xo	CF	52.0
" "	22	Tu	18-Jun-96	Bridgwater	Plymouth	1V29	2350WloPnz	xo	CF	92.3
" "	23	Tu	02-Jul-96	Exeter	Paddington	1A19	0555PlyPad	xo	CF	173.4
" "	24	Mo	23-Mar-98	Yeovil Pen Mill	Exeter	1V29	2350WloPnz	xo	CF	51.1
" "	25	Fr	27-Mar-98	Starcross	Newton Abbot	1V57	0910AbdPly	xo	CF	11.7
" "	26	Sa	04-Apr-98	Exeter	Penzance	1V29	2350WloPnz	xo	CF	131.6
" "	27	Th	23-Apr-98	Teignmouth	Bristol	1E31	0826PgnNcl	xo	CF	90.5
37203	1	Sa	09-May-81	Plymouth	Penzance	2B36	1745PlyPnz	xo	LA	79.5
" "	2	Sa	16-May-81	Plymouth	Penzance	2B36	1745PlyPnz	xo	LA	79.5
" "	3	Fr	22-May-81	Par	Plymouth	1E21	1025PnzLds	xo	LA	34.8
" "	4	Sa	23-May-81	Plymouth	Penzance	2B36	1745PlyPnz	xo	LA	79.5
" "	5	Th	24-Mar-88	Honiton	Exeter	1V12	1203PshPgn	xo	IM?	17.4

Loco	log	dy	date	from	to	code	train	detail		miles
" "	6	Tu	28-Sep-93	Exeter	Plymouth	1V48	1018LvpPly	xo	BR	52.0
" "	7	Tu	28-Sep-93	Plymouth	Bristol	1E39	1700PlyLds	xo	BR	127.5
37204	1	Tu	04-Mar-86	Bristol	Exeter	1C09	0635BtmPly	xo	BR	76.5
" "	2	Th	22-May-86	Treverrin tunnel	Plymouth	1E91	0933PnzNcl	xo	BR	32.0
" "	3	Sa	14-Jun-86	Par	Plymouth		2105ParPly	xo	BR	34.8
37206	1	Su	22-Nov-81	Par ?	Plymouth	1A07	2135PnzPad	xo	LA	34.8
" "	2	We	11-Aug-82	Plymouth	Lostwithiel	2B87	1620PlyNqy	xo	CF	30.3
37207	1	Su	11-Oct-80	Plymouth	Lostwithiel	2B12	1000PlyPnz	xo	LA	49.2
" "	2	Sa	07-Aug-82	?	Plymouth		0918EdbPly	xo	LA	
" "	3	Th	11-Aug-82	Lostwithiel	Newquay		1620PlyNqy	xo	LA	25.2
" "	4	Su	30-Jan-83	Exeter	Plymouth		1230EdbPly	xo	LA	52.0
" "	5	Sa	16-Jul-83	Par	Newquay	2B87	0712ParNqy	xo	LA	20.8
" "	6	Sa	16-Jul-83	Newquay	Par	2B87	0810NqyPar	xo	LA	20.8
" "	7	Sa	16-Jul-83	Par	Newquay	2B87	1305ParNqy	xo	LA	20.8
" "	8	Sa	16-Jul-83	Newquay	Par	2B87	1405NqyPar	xo	LA	20.8
" "	9	Sa	16-Jul-83	Par	Newquay	2B87	1645ParNqy	xo	LA	20.8
" "	10	Sa	16-Jul-83	Newquay	Par	2B87	1740NqyPar	xo	LA	20.8
" "	11	Sa	16-Jul-83	Par	Newquay	2B87	1955ParNqy	xo	LA	20.8
" "	12	Sa	16-Jul-83	Newquay	Par	2B47	2110NqyPar	xo	LA	20.8
" "	13	Su	17-Jul-83	Par	Newquay	2B87	1205ParNqy	xo	LA	20.8
" "	14	Su	17-Jul-83	Newquay	Par	2B87	1340NqyPar	xo	LA	20.8
" "	15	Su	17-Jul-83	Par	Newquay	2B87	1510ParNqy	xo	LA	20.8
" "	16	Su	17-Jul-83	Newquay	Par	2B87	1610NqyPar	xo	LA	20.8
" "	17	Su	17-Jul-83	Par	Newquay	2B87	1715ParNqy	xo	LA	20.8
" "	18	Su	17-Jul-83	Newquay	Par	2B87	1858NqyPar	xo	LA	20.8
" "	19	Mo	29-Aug-83	Lostwithiel	Penzance	1V76	0920LvpPnz	xo	LA	49.2
" "	20	Tu	05-Feb-83	Par	Plymouth	1A02	2135PnzPad	xo	LA	34.8
" "	21	Tu	14-May-84	Par	Penzance		?	xo	LA	34.8
" "	22	Su	22-Jul-84	Par	Newquay	2B87	1510ParNqy	xo	LA	20.8
" "	23	Su	22-Jul-84	Newquay	Par	2B87	1650NqyPar	xo	LA	20.8
" "	24	Su	22-Jul-84	Par	Newquay	2B87	1815ParNqy	xo	LA	20.8
" "	25	Su	22-Jul-84	Newquay	Par	2B87	1950NqyPar	xo	LA	20.8
" "	26	Sa	11-Aug-84	St Germans	Liskeard	1V64	0717DbyPnz	xo	LA	9.5
" "	27	Sa	25-Aug-84	Plymouth	Exeter	1A79	1448PnzPad	xo	LA	52.0
" "	28	Sa	17-Aug-85	Menheniot	Penzance	1C21	0805SwaPnz	xo	LA	64.9
" "	29	Th	05-Jun-86	Newton Abbot	Plymouth	1V65	0943NclPnz	xo	LA	31.9
" "	30	We	26-Nov-86	Lostwithiel	Plymouth	1A50	1000PnzPad	xo	LA	30.3
" "	31	Sa	07-Feb-87	Liskeard	Penzance	1C11	0645SdnPnz	xo	LA	61.8
" "	32	Sa	07-Feb-87	Penzance	Par	1F84	1412PnzBtm	xo	LA	34.8
" "	33	We	22-Jul-87	Penzance	Par	1F88	1830PnzBtm	xo	LA	34.8
" "	34	Sa	01-Aug-87	Par	Plymouth	1M45	1133PnzLvp	xo	LA	34.8
" "	35	Fr	18-Sep-87	Truro	Plymouth	2C89	1950PnzPly	xo	LA	53.6
" "	36	Fr	02-Oct-87	Exeter	Barnstaple	1C07	0405ExdBpl	xo	LA	38.9
" "	37	Fr	02-Oct-87	Barnstaple	Exeter	2C68	0545BplPnz	xo	LA	38.9
" "	38	Th	17-Mar-88	Exeter	Plymouth		1445PadPly	xo	LA	52.0
" "	39	Sa	01-Jun-91	Newton Abbot	Plymouth	1V32	2055GgcPly	xo	CF	31.9
" "	40	Sa	27-Jul-91	Paignton	Bristol	1M10	1705PgnMcp	xo	CF	103.8
" "	41	Su	02-Feb-92	Exeter	Plymouth	1C34	1020PadPnz	xo	CF	52.0

Loco	log	dy	date	from	to	code	train		detail	miles
" "	42	Fr	21-Feb-92	Exeter	Newton Abbot	2C59	2210ExdNab	xo	CF	20.2
" "	43	Sa	22-Feb-92	Exeter	Plymouth	1V38	0605LdsPly	xo	CF	52.0
" "	44	Sa	22-Feb-92	Exeter	Salisbury	1O41	1622ExdWlo	xo	CF	88.7
" "	45	Mo	05-Sep-94	Exeter	Bristol		0620PlyNcl	xo	CF	75.5
" "	46	We	19-Oct-94	Exeter	Bristol	1M48	1545PlyDby	xo	CF	52.0
37208	1	Th	09-Apr-81	Plymouth ?	Exeter	1A79	1008PnzPad	xo	BR	52.0
" "	2	Sa	30-Jan-82	Plymouth ?	Exeter	1A59	0900PnzPad	xo	BR	52.0
" "	3	Tu	15-Apr-86	Bristol	Exeter	1C09	0635BtmPly	xo	BR	76.5
37211	1	Mo	19-Sep-88	Pewsey	Exeter	1C45	1302PadPly	xo	SF	98.1
37213	1	Sa	05-Mar-94	Exeter	Bristol	1M56	1015PlyMcp	xo	BR	75.5
" "	2	Sa	25-Jun-94	Exeter	Paignton	1V46	0605GgcPgn	xo	TO	28.3
" "	3	Sa	25-Jun-94	Paignton	Bristol	1M48	1603PgnLvp	xo	TO	103.8
" "	4	We	23-Aug-95	Exeter	Plymouth	1V38	0605LdsPly	xo	CF	52.0
" "	5	Su	03-Sep-95	Exeter	Penzance	1C52	1410PadPnz	xo	CF	131.6
" "	6	We	06-Sep-95	Powderham	Exeter	1E40	1650PlySfd	xo	CF	6.0
" "	7	We	24-Apr-96	Exeter	Plymouth	1C76	1935PadPly	xo	CF	52.0
" "	8	Th	25-Apr-96	Plymouth	Exeter	1O03	2215PnzWlo	xo	CF	52.0
37214	1	Tu	04-Aug-87	Cheltenham	Plymouth	1V68	1125NclPnz	xo	CF	171.9
" "	2	Sa	18-Nov-95	Exeter	Plymouth	1V39	0605LdsPly	xo	CF	52.0
37215	1	Tu	27-Feb-90	Exeter	Plymouth		1618McpPly	xo	CF	52.0
37217	1	Fr	06-Mar-87	Bristol	Exeter	1C09	0635BtmPly	xo	CF	76.5
37219	1	Sa	22-Sep-84	Birmingham	Paignton	1V71	0820LvpPgn	xo	MR	193.9
" "	2	Sa	22-Sep-84	Paignton	Birmingham	1M65	1608PgnLvp	xo	MR	193.9
" "	3	Sa	02-Oct-93	Newton Abbot	Bristol	1S93	1518PgnGgc	xo	SF	95.7
" "	4	Fr	25-Feb-94	Exeter	Penzance	1C40	1335PadPnz	xo	SF	131.6
" "	5	Tu	19-Jan-99	Exeter	Bristol	1M40	1140PlyLvp	xo	TO	76.5
37222	1	We	06-Nov-85	Largin	Plymouth	1A85	1617PnzPad	xo	LA	22.9
" "	2	We	20-Nov-85	Largin	Plymouth	1S71	0730PnzAbd	xo	LA	22.9
" "	3	Tu	09-Nov-93	Exeter	Plymouth	1C32	1235PadPnz	xo	CF	52.0
37223	1	We	25-Aug-93	Taunton	Plymouth	1V33	2300GgcPly	xo	BR	80.7
37225	1	Tu	16-Dec-97	Exeter	Plymouth	1V35	0604DbyPly	xo	IM	52.0
" "	2	Tu	16-Dec-97	Plymouth	Exeter	1M40	1140PlyLvp	xo	IM	52.0
37227	1	Su	21-Mar-93	Exeter	Penzance	1C53	1415PadPnz	xo	CF	131.6
37229	1	Th	16-Mar-95	Par	Penzance		1335PadPnz	xo	CF	34.8
" "	2	Sa	30-Dec-95	Exeter	Plymouth	1V63	1500NclPly	xo	CF	52.0
" "	3	Mo	01-Jan-96	Exeter	Plymouth	1C50	1535PadPnz	xo	CF	52.0
" "	4	Tu	30-Jan-96	Exeter	Plymouth	1V29	2350WloPnz	xo	CF	52.0
" "	5	Tu	30-Jan-96	Exeter	Bristol	1M56	1044PlyMcp	xo	CF	75.5
" "	6	Mo	05-Feb-96	Exeter	Plymouth	1V56	0910LvpPly	xo	CF	52.0
" "	7	Fr	21-Feb-97	Torquay	Bristol East Yard	1E31	0826PgnNcl	xo	CF	102.7
" "	8	Fr	15-Aug-97	Plymouth	Taunton	1M40	1140PlyLvp	xo	CF	82.8
" "	9	Tu	06-Apr-99	Exeter	Plymouth	1V38	0605LdsPly	xo	TO	52.0
" "	10	Tu	06-Apr-99	Plymouth	Exeter	1E36	1300PlyLds	xo	TO	52.0
37230	1	Fr	01-May-92	Exeter	Plymouth	1C44	1435PadPnz	xo	CF	52.0
" "	2	Sa	16-May-92	Par	Plymouth	1C51	1935PnzPly	xo	CF	34.8
" "	3	Fr	22-May-92	Cowley Bridge	Exeter	1V59	0912AbdPnz	xo	CF	1.3
" "	4	Sa	13-Jun-92	Crewkerne	Exeter	1V10	1047BskPgn	xo	CF	40.7
" "	5	Mo	22-Jun-92	Topsham	Exeter		1850ExmExd	xo	CF	6.2

Loco	log	dy	date	from	to	code	train		detail	miles
" "	6	Sa	04-Jul-92	Paignton	Bristol	1S93	1530PgnGgc	xo	CF	103.8
" "	7	Sa	04-Jul-92	Exeter	Taunton	1A91	1638PnzPad	xo	CF	30.8
" "	8	Th	09-Jul-92	Exeter	Salisbury	1O41	1622ExdWlo	xo	CF	88.7
" "	9	Th	09-Jul-92	Salisbury	Exeter	1V19	1815WloExd	xo	CF	88.7
" "	10	Mo	10-Aug-92	Crewkerne	Exeter	1V09	0835WloExd	xo	CF	40.7
" "	11	Su	15-Dec-96	Exeter	Plymouth	1C72	1835PadPly	xo	CF	52.0
" "	12	Th	27-Feb-97	Plymouth	Bristol	1E40	1650PlySfd	xo	CF	127.5
" "	13	Su	02-Nov-97	Exeter	Plymouth	1V52	1005NclPly	xo	CF	52.0
" "	14	Tu	11-Nov-97	Exeter	Birmingham	1M56	1040PlyMcp	xo	CF	166.6
37232	1	Fr	14-Feb-86	Bristol	Exeter	1C09	0635BtmPly	xo	BR	76.5
" "	2	Fr	21-Mar-86	Bristol	Exeter	1C09	0635BtmPly	xo	BR	76.5
" "	3	Fr	06-May-88	Yeovil Jn	Exeter	1V19	1910WloExd	xo	BR	49.6
37233	1	We	08-Oct-80	Par ?	Penzance	1V76	0920LvpPnz	xo	BR	44.8
" "	2	Tu	28-Aug-84	Paignton	Birmingham	1Z18	1715PgnBns	xo	BR	193.9
37235	1	Tu	21-Jan-86	Bristol	Exeter	1C09	0635BtmPly	xo	BR	76.5
" "	2	Mo	03-Nov-86	Largin	Plymouth	1S71	0730PnzAbd	xo	LA	22.9
" "	3	Fr	20-Mar-87	Lostwithiel	Plymouth	2C84	1203PnzPly	xo	LA	30.3
" "	4	We	25-Mar-87	Plymouth	Penzance	2C74	1635PlyPnz	xo	LA	79.5
" "	5	Sa	11-Apr-87	Penzance	Plymouth		1626PnzPly	xo	LA	79.5
" "	6	We	10-Jun-87	Penzance	Plymouth	2C83	0911PnzPly	xo	LA	79.5
37239	1	Th	10-Oct-85	Bristol	Plymouth	1Z90	1736BtmPly	xo	CF	127.5
" "	2	Mo	06-Feb-89	Axminster	Yeovil Jn		1100ExdWlo	xo	CF	21.9
" "	3	Mo	06-Feb-89	Chard Jn	Axminster	1V13	1310WloExd	xo	CF	5.1
37246	1	Fr	05-Jul-85	York	Plymouth		1425YrkPly	xo	TI	348.6
37247	1	Sa	11-Aug-84	St Germans	Liskeard	1V64	0717DbyPnz	xb	LA	9.5
" "	2		??-Sep-85	Par	Plymouth	1A85	1610PnzPad	xb	I A	34.8
37248	1	Mo	26-Jun-89	Exeter	Plymouth		2200PadPly	xo	CF	52.0
37250	1	Sa	04-Jul-87	Exeter	Paignton	1V29	2250GgcPgn	xo	CF	28.3
" "	2	Sa	04-Jul-87	Paignton	Exeter	1S64	1015PgnGgc	xo	CF	28.3
37251	1	Tu	31-Jul-84	York	Plymouth		1030YrkPly	xo	CF	341.9
37254	1	Sa	10-Aug-91	Lavington	Penzance	1C27	1030PadPnz	xo	CF	218.3
" "	2	Th	14-Jul-94	Totnes	Plymouth	1C76	1935PadPly	xo	CF	23.2
" "	3	Tu	18-Oct-94	Hackney Yard	Newton Abbot	1V48	1217McpPly	xo	CF	0.5
" "	4	We	08-May-96	Bristol	Plymouth	1V48	1217McpPly	xo	CF	127.5
" "	5	Fr	17-May-96	Exeter	Penzance	1V52	0850EdbPnz	xo	CF	131.6
" "	6	Fr	26-Jul-96	Exeter	Penzance	1C28	1045PadPnz	xo	CF	131.6
" "	7	Tu	06-Aug-96	Ivybridge	Birmingham	1M56	1044PlyMcp	xo	CF	206.9
" "	8	We	01-Jan-97	Exeter	Bristol	1M56	1044PlyMcp	xo	CF	75.5
" "	9	Mo	06-Jan-97	Exeter	Bristol	1O03	2215PnzWlo	xo	CF	75.5
" "	10	We	15-Jan-97	Exeter	Plymouth	1C82	2035PadPly	xo	CF	52.0
37258	1	Fr	23-Aug-91	Totnes	Plymouth		0735PadPly	xo	CF	22.2
" "	2	Fr	23-Aug-91	Plymouth	Waterloo	1O40	1355PlyWlo	xo	CF	224.4
" "	3	Fr	23 Aug 91	Waterloo	Exeter	2V21	1915WloExd	xo	CF	172.4
" "	4	Su	22-Sep-91	Exeter	Bristol	1S19	2100PlyEdb	xo	CF	75.5
" "	5	Sa	23-Jan-93	Exeter	Salisbury		0811ExdBsk	xo	CF	88.7
" "	6	Sa	23-Jan-93	Salisbury	Exeter	1V09	0915WloExd	xo	CF	88.7
" "	7	Tu	26-Jan-93	Taunton	Plymouth	1V59	0912AbdPly	xo	CF	82.8
" "	8	We	27-Jan-93	Exeter	Plymouth		1145PadPnz	xo	CF	52.0

Loco	log	dy	date	from	to	code	train	detail		miles
" "	9	Tu	09-Feb-93	Crewkerne	Exeter	2V13	1315WloExd	xo	CF	40.7
" "	10	Sa	13-Aug-94	Exeter	Reading	1A16	0643ExdRdg	xo	CF	137.5
" "	11	Tu	23-Aug-94	Exeter	Bristol	1Z37	1448NabBtm	xo	CF	75.5
" "	12	Tu	20-Dec-94	Exeter	Plymouth	1C22	0945PadPly	xo	CF	52.0
" "	13	Sa	18-Mar-95	Tiverton Pkwy.	Bristol	1M48	1545PlyDby	xo	CF	45.0
" "	14	Th	13-Apr-95	Paignton	Exeter	1E37	1430PgnNcl	xo	CF	28.3
37263	1	Su	07-Jul-91	Exeter	Plymouth	1C76	1935PadPnz	xi	CF	52.0
" "	2	Mo	02-Mar-92	Exeter	Plymouth	1V53	2120GgcPly	xi	CF	52.0
" "	3	Fr	06-Mar-92	Exeter	Bristol	1A03	2215PnzPad	xi	CF	75.5
" "	4	Sa	18-Sep-93	Paignton	Bristol	1M42	1611PgnLvp	xi	CF	103.8
" "	5	Mo	11-Jul-94	Exeter	Plymouth	1C02	2355PadPnz	xi	CF	52.0
" "	6	Mo	11-Jul-94	Ivybridge	Totnes		0735PlyPad	xi	CF	10.0
" "	7	Sa	16-Jul-94	Exeter	Paignton	1V50	1217McpPgn	xi	CF	28.3
" "	8	Tu	21-Nov-95	Exeter	Plymouth	1V50	0640DdePnz	xi	CF	52.0
" "	9	Tu	21-Nov-95	Exeter	Plymouth	1V57	0910AbdPly	xi	CF	52.0
" "	10	Fr	02-Aug-96	Exeter	Plymouth	1C36	1235PadPnz	xi	CF	52.0
" "	11	Su	18-Aug-96	Exeter	Plymouth	1V46	0924LdsPly	xi	CF	52.0
" "	12	Su	18-Aug-96	Plymouth	Exeter	1C68	1815PlyBtm	xi	CF	52.0
" "	13	Mo	24-Nov-97	Truro	Penzance	1V29	2350WloPnz	xi	CF	28.0
37264	1	Fr	08-Apr-94	Exeter	Plymouth	1V56	1205NclPly	xi	TO	52.0
" "	2	Th	12-Aug-99	Plymouth	Bristol	1S35	0922PnzEdb	xi	TO	127.5
37266	1	Sa	25-Aug-84	Sheffield	Paignton	1V49	1521SfdPgn	xb	LE	271.5
37267	1	Sa	16-Jun-79	Par	Penzance	1B44	0930PadPnz	xb	LA	44.8
" "	2	We	25-Jul-79	Paignton	Plymouth	2B16	1000PgnPly	xb	LA	39.9
" "	3	Tu	14-Aug-79	Totnes	Exeter	1M74	1356PnzBns	xb	LA	28.9
" "	4	Fr	01-Mar-85	Bristol	Exeter	1C09	0635BtmPly	xb	LE	75.5
37269	1	Mo	09-Apr-84	Plymouth	Bristol	1M85	0740PnzLvp	xo	CF	127.5
37270	1	Su	10-Jul-83	Par	Newquay		1715ParNqy	xo	LA	20.8
" "	2	Su	10-Jul-83	Newquay	Par		1858NqyPar	xo	LA	20.8
" "	3	Sa	16-Jul-83	Truro	Plymouth	1E61	1815PnzBtm	xo	LA	53.6
37272	1	Su	25-Sep-83	Par ?	Exeter	1A07	2135PnzPad	xo	LA	86.8
37273	1	Sa	07-Jul-84	Penzance	Plymouth	1M44	1125PnzMcp	xo	LA	79.5
" "	2	We	01-Aug-84	Newquay	Plymouth	2C83	0950NqyPly	xo	LA	55.5
37274	1	Su	22-Nov-81	Par ?	Plymouth	1A07	2135PnzPad	xo	LA	34.8
" "	2	Sa	14-Aug-82	Par	Newquay		xxxx NqyPar	xo	LA	20.8
" "	3	Sa	14-Aug-82	Newquay	Par		xxxx ParNqy	xo	LA	20.8
" "	4	Sa	04-Sep-82	Plymouth	Exeter	1A13	1045PnzPad	xo	LA	52.0
" "	5	Su	12-Dec-82	Par ?	Exeter	1A07	2135PnzPad	xo	LA	86.8
37275	1	Sa	23-Jun-84	Birmingham	Paignton	1V71	0820LvpPgn	xo	CF	193.9
" "	2	Sa	23-Jun-84	Paignton	Birmingham	1M65	1608PgnLvp	xo	CF	193.9
" "	3	Fr	24-Aug-84	Bristol	Plymouth	1V49	1420YrkPly	xo	CF	127.5
" "	4	Th	04-Sep-97	Plymouth	Newton Abbot	1M40	1140PlyLvp	xo	CF	31.9
" "	5	Sa	13-Dec-97	Exeter	Newton Abbot	1C50	1535PadPnz	xo	CF	20.2
" "	6	We	17-Dec-97	Bridgwater	Plymouth	1V63	1502NclPly	xo	CF	93.0
37281	1	Sa	10-Nov-84	Par	Penzance	2C68	0545BplPnz	xo	LA	44.8
" "	2	Su	11-Nov-84	Par	Plymouth	1A07	2135PnzPad	xo	LA	34.8
37298	1	Fr	04-Jun-99	St Austell	Penzance	1C42	1432PadPnz	xo	TO	40.2
37299	1	Fr	08-Aug-80	Par	Plymouth	1E61	1808PnzLds	xo	LA	34.8

Loco	log	dy	date	from	to	code	train	detail		miles
" "	2	Tu	25-Nov-80	Par	Exeter	1A59	1332PnzPad	xo	LA	86.8
" "	3	Sa	13-Jun-81	Penzance	Plymouth	1M83	1050PnzMcp	xo	LA	44.7
" "	4	Sa	04-Sep-82	Plymouth	Exeter	1A13	1045PnzPad	xo	LA	52.0
" "	5	Fr	27-Jul-84	Bristol	Silk Mill		1030YrkPly	xo	BR	46.1
37307	1	Sa	09-Jun-84	Penzance	Plymouth	1Z26	0545PnzWem	xo	LE	79.5
" "	2	Mo	20-Aug-84	Par	Newquay		1138ParNqy	xo	LE	20.8
" "	3	Mo	20-Aug-84	Newquay	Par		1325NqyPar	xo	LE	20.8
" "	4	Mo	20-Aug-84	Par	Penzance	1V81	0922LdsPnz	xo	LE	44.8
37350	1	Sa	12-Jun-99	Bristol	Paignton	1V26	2330McpPgn	xo	TO	103.8
" "	2	Sa	12-Jun-99	Paignton	Bristol	1S66	0858PgnGgc	xo	TO	104.8
37351	1	Fr	07-May-99	Plymouth	Bristol	1M56	0848PnzMcp	xo	TO	127.5
37357	1	Su	29-Oct-89	Newton Abbot	Plymouth	1C28	0940PadPnz	xo	TI	31.9
" "	2	Mo	30-Oct-89	Plymouth	Exeter	1A03	2145PnzPad	xo	TI	52.0
37359	1	Tu	29-Jan-91	Lostwithiel	Penzance	1C02	2355PadPnz	xi	TE	49.2
37372	1	We	04-Sep-91	Exeter	Bristol	1S19	2100PlyEdb	xo	CF	75.5
" "	2	We	19-Feb-92	Exeter	Basingstoke	1O44	1940ExdBsk	xo	CF	124.6
" "	3	Su	13-Sep-92	Exeter	Salisbury	1O41	1607ExdWlo	xo	CF	88.7
" "	4	Su	13-Sep-92	Salisbury	Exeter	1V19	1855WloExd	xo	CF	88.7
37407	1	Sa	15-Apr-95	Cardiff	Paignton	1C21	1000CdfPgn	xe	CD	142.9
" "	2	Sa	15-Apr-95	Paignton	Bristol	1B33	1332PgnBtm	xe	CD	104.8
" "	3	Th	20-Apr-95	Bristol	Paignton	1C21	1048BtmPgn	xe	CD	104.8
" "	4	Th	20-Apr-95	Paignton	Bristol	1B33	1332PgnBtm	xe	CD	104.8
37408	1	Tu	23-Dec-93	Westbury	Exeter	1C02	2355PadPnz	xe	CD	82.4
37411	1	Fr	08-Feb-91	Exeter	Plymouth	1Z33	0752ExdPly	xe	LA	52.0
" "	2	Sa	09-Feb-91	Exeter	Plymouth	2C66	0915ExdPnz	xe	LA	52.0
" "	3	Sa	28-Sep-91	Totnes	Plymouth	1V33	2120GgcPly	xe	LA	23.2
" "	4	Sa	20-Jun-92	Lostwithiel	Penzance		2115NclPnz	xe	LA	49.2
" "	5	Fr	17-Jul-92	Menheniot	Penzance	1C02	0005PadPnz	xe	LA	64.9
" "	6	Sa	23-Jan-93	Exeter	Basingstoke	1O37	1225ExdBsk	xe	LA	124.6
" "	7	Sa	23-Jan-93	Basingstoke	Exeter	1V17	1802BskExd	xe	LA	124.6
" "	8	We	14-Aug-96	Exeter	Paignton	1Z70	0855ExdPgn	xe	CF	28.3
" "	9	We	14-Aug-96	Paignton	Bristol	1Z71	1631PgnBtm	xe	CF	104.8
" "	10	Sa	17-Aug-96	Cardiff	Paignton	1C17	0915CdfPgn	xe	CF	142.9
" "	11	Sa	17-Aug-96	Paignton	Cardiff	1B32	1332PgnCdf	xe	CF	142.9
37412	1	Sa	03-Jun-89	Par	Newquay		.... PadNqy	xe	LA	20.8
" "	2	We	07-Feb-90	Exeter	Plymouth		1635PadPly	xe	LA	52.0
" "	3	Sa	28-Sep-91	Par	Exeter		0940NqyEdb	xe	LA	86.8
" "	4	Fr	15-May-92	Truro	Plymouth	1A91	1630PnzPad	xe	LA	53.6
" "	5	Th	17-Feb-94	Par	Penzance	1C02	2355PadPnz	xe	LA	44.8
" "	6	Sa	24-May-97	Cardiff	Paignton	1C17	0915CdfPgn	xe	CF	142.8
" "	7	Sa	24-May-97	Paignton	Cardiff	1B32	1330PgnCdf	xe	CF	142.8
37413	1	Sa	22-Aug-92	Par	Newquay	1V26	2355LdsNqy	xe	LA	20.8
" "	2	Sa	22-Aug-92	Newquay	Par	1M62	0815NqyMcp	xe	LA	20.8
" "	3	Th	15-Sep-94	Liskeard	Penzance	1C28	1035PadPnz	xe	LA	61.8
" "	4	Tu	12 Dec-95	Bristol	Paignton	1C21	1054BtmPgn	xe	CF	104.8
" "	5	Tu	12-Dec-95	Paignton	Bristol	1B33	1332PgnBtm	xe	CF	104.8
37414	1	We	31-May-89	Plymouth	Exeter	1A02	2045PnzPad	xe	LA	52.0
" "	2	Fr	03-Aug-90	Par?	Plymouth		1330PnzPly?	xe	LA	34.8

Loco	log	dy	date	from	to	code	train	detail		miles
" "	3	Sa	04-Aug-90	Par	Plymouth		1440PnzMcp	xe	LA	34.8
37416	1	We	10-Aug-94	Par	Penzance		0005PadPnz	xe	CF	44.8
37417	1	We	06-Nov-91	Bodmin Parkway	Plymouth	1A48	0847PnzPad	xe	LA	26.9
37418	1	Tu	11-Jan-94	Bristol	Paignton	1C21	1000CdfPgn	xe	CD	104.8
" "	2	Tu	11-Jan-94	Paignton	Bristol	1B40	1345PgnCdf	xe	CD	104.8
37419	1	Fr	06-Sep-91	Exeter	Yeovil Jn	2O04	1738ExdWlo	xe	TI	49.6
" "	2	Su	08-Sep-91	Exeter	Basingstoke	2O05	2040ExdBsk	xe	TI	124.6
37420	1	We	06-Nov-91	Bodmin Parkway	Plymouth	1A48	0847PnzPad	xe	LA	26.9
37422	1	Tu	15-Feb-94	Bristol	Paignton	1C21	1048BtmPgn	xe	CD	104.8
" "	2	Tu	15-Feb-94	Paignton	Bristol	1B40	1340PgnBtm	xe	CD	104.8
37425	1	Sa	04-Sep-04	Plymouth	Birmingham	1M25	1420NqyMcp	xe	MG	217.7
37426	1	Th	19-Nov-87	Bristol	Exeter	1C80	2235BtmExd	xe	CF	76.5
37427	1	Tu	17-Feb-87	Bristol	Exeter	1C09	0635BtmPly	xe	CF	76.5
37503	1	Sa	25-Jul-98	Newton Abbot	Plymouth	1V29	2350WloPnz	xo	TO	31.9
37513	1	Th	15-Oct-98	Exeter	Bristol	1E36	1300PlyNcl	xo	IM	75.5
37521	1	Tu	07-Nov-95	Exeter	Plymouth	1C36	1235PadPnz	xo	CF	52.0
" "	2	Th	06-Jun-96	Exeter	Leeds	1E39	1607ExdLds	xo	CF	291.5
" "	3	Tu	08-Oct-96	Exeter	Plymouth	1V63	1500NclPly	xo	CF	52.0
" "	4	Tu	14-Oct-97	Exeter	Plymouth	1V56	1203NclPly	xo	CF	52.0
37668	1	Fr	05-Jun-98	Truro	Plymouth	1O03	2200PnzWlo	xo	CF	53.6
37669	1	Fr	12-Aug-88	Exeter	Plymouth	1V54	1325LvpPly	xo	LA	52.0
" "	2	Sa	21-Jul-90	Par	Bristol	1S04	1000PnzEdb	xo	LA	162.3
" "	3	Tu	02-Feb-99	Redruth	Penzance	1V50	0840GgcPnz	xo	TO	16.8
37670	1	Fr	23-Oct-87	Liskeard	Penzance	1V59	0720GgcPnz	xo	LA	61.8
" "	2	Tu	10-Nov-87	Largin	Plymouth	1F88	1830PnzBtm	xo	LA	22.9
" "	3	Tu	10-Nov-87	Par	Plymouth	1A02	2135PnzPad	xo	LA	34.8
" "	4	Sa	12-Aug-89	Truro	Plymouth	1S71	0817PnzGgc	xo	LA	53.6
" "	5	Sa	26-Aug-89	Bodmin Parkway	Exeter	1A44	0735PnzPad	xo	LA	79.0
" "	6	Sa	21-Oct-89	Penzance	Exeter	1A56	0955PnzPad	xo	LA	131.6
" "	7	We	07-Feb-90	Exeter	Plymouth	1C54	1635PadPly	xo	LA	52.0
" "	8	Sa	14-Dec-91	Par	Plymouth		1905PnzPly	xo	LA	34.8
" "	9	Sa	08-Aug-92	Par	Newquay	1V37?	0655McpNqy	xo	LA	20.8
" "	10	Sa	08-Aug-92	Newquay	Plymouth	1E44	1440NqyLds	xo	LA	55.5
" "	11	Sa	15-Jun-96	Par	Newquay	1V39	0605LdsNqy	xo	CF	20.8
" "	12	Sa	15-Jun-96	Newquay	Par	1E39	1408NqyLds	xo	CF	20.8
" "	13	Th	03-Oct-96	Exeter	Plymouth	1V63	1500NclPly	xo	CF	52.0
" "	14	Mo	07-Oct-96	Bridgwater	Exeter	1V48	1217McpPly	xo	CF	42.3
" "	15	Mo	10-May-99	Par	Penzance	1C00	2350PadPnz	xo	TO	44.8
" "	16	Sa	14-Sep-02	Exeter	Plymouth	1C65	1733Pad-Ply	xo	CD	8.7
37671	1	We	15-Jul-87	Bristol	Exeter	1C80	2235BtmExd	xo	LA	76.5
" "	2	Sa	01-Apr-89	Par	Plymouth		1730PnzBtm	xo	LA	34.8
" "	3	Sa	12-Aug 89	Truro	Plymouth	1S71	0817PnzGgc	xo	LA	53.6
" "	4	Th	25-Jan-90	Newton Abbot	Exeter		1800NabExd	xo	LA	20.2
" "	5	Sa	18-Aug-90	Par	Exeter	1A58	1130NqyPad	xo	LA	86.8
" "	6	Sa	13-Jun-92	Exeter	Plymouth	1V47	1018McpPnz	xo	LA	52.0
" "	7	Su	14-Jun-92	Exeter	Plymouth	1C72	1835PadPly	xo	LA	52.0

Loco	log	dy	date	from	to	code	train	detail		miles
" "	8	Mo	07-Sep-92	Chard Jn	Exeter	1V19	1815WloExd	xo	LA	32.8
" "	9	We	20-Mar-96	Bodmin Parkway	Plymouth	1S71	0720PnzEdb	xo	CF	26.9
" "	10	Th	03-Oct-96	Exeter	Plymouth	1V63	1500NclPly	xo	CF	52.0
" "	11	Sa	22-Nov-97	Plymouth	Bristol	1S35	0922PnzEdb	xo	CF	127.5
37672	1	Mo	07-Dec-87	Truro	Plymouth	1F88	1830PnzBtm	xo	LA	53.6
" "	2	Mo	29-Feb-88	Newton Abbot	Exeter	2C37	0817PgnExd	xo	LA	20.2
" "	3	Sa	16-Jul-88	Truro	Plymouth	1E36	1117PnzNcl	xo	LA	53.6
" "	4	Sa	26-Aug-89	Bodmin Parkway	Exeter	1A44	0735PnzPad	xo	LA	79.0
" "	5	Sa	07-Jul-90	Newquay	Exeter		0815NqyMcp	xo	LA	107.6
" "	6	Su	21-Jun-92	Exeter	Paignton	1Z22	0800PadPgn	xo	LA	28.3
" "	7	Su	21-Jun-92	Paignton	Exeter	1Z22	1805PgnPad	xo	LA	28.3
" "	8	Sa	08-Aug-92	Par	Newquay	1V37?	0655McpNqy	xo	LA	20.8
" "	9	Sa	08-Aug-92	Newquay	Plymouth	1E44	1440NqyLds	xo	LA	55.5
" "	10	Sa	22-Aug-92	Par	Exeter	1M62	0815NqyMcp	xo	LA	86.8
" "	11	Su	01-Oct-95	Par	Penzance	1C50	1535PadPnz	xo	CF	44.8
" "	12	We	01-Jul-98	Exeter	Plymouth	1V35	0636WptPly	xo	CF	52.0
" "	13	We	01-Jul-98	Plymouth	Exeter	1M40	1140PlyMcp	xo	CF	52.0
37673	1	Th	12-Nov-87	Plymouth	Newton Abbot	1A02	2135PnzPad	xo	LA	31.9
" "	2	Sa	20-Feb-88	St Austell	Penzance	2C68	0702ExdPnz	xo	LA	40.2
" "	3	Sa	20-Feb-88	Penzance	Plymouth	2C84	1213PnzPly	xo	LA	79.5
" "	4	Su	31-Jul-88	Newton Abbot	Plymouth		2140PadPly	xo	LA	31.9
" "	5	Sa	27-May-89	Par	Newquay		0915PlyNqy	xo	LA	20.8
" "	6	Sa	27-May-89	Newquay	Exeter	1A61	1105NqyPad	xo	LA	107.6
" "	7	Fr	20-Apr-90	Bristol	Exeter		1722BtmExd	xo	LA	76.5
" "	8	Su	15-Dec-91	Hemerdon	Bristol	1S91	1308PlmEdb	xo	LA	120.8
" "	9	We	11-Dec-96	Par	Penzance	1V29	2350WloPnz	xo	CF	44.8
" "	10	Su	16-Nov-97	Lostwithiel	Plymouth	1S91	1053PnzEdb	xo	CF	30.3
" "	11	Sa	22-Nov-97	Plymouth	Bristol	1S35	0922PnzEdb	xo	CF	127.5
" "	12	Mo	01-Dec-97	Exeter	Plymouth	1V63	1502NclPly	xo	CF	52.0
" "	13	We	03-Dec-97	Plymouth	Exeter	1S35	0922PnzEdb	xo	CF	52.0
37674	1	We	01-Jul-87	Truro	Plymouth	2C89	1950PnzPly	xo	LA	53.6
" "	2	Sa	29-Aug-87	Par	Penzance	1V53	0816LvpPnz	xo	LA	34.8
" "	3	Fr	26-Feb-88	Truro	Penzance	1V59	0720GgcPnz	xo	LA	25.9
" "	4	Su	05-Jun-88	Truro	Par	1S87	1055PnzAbd	xo	LA	18.9
" "	5	Su	31-Jul-88	Newton Abbot	Plymouth		2140PadPly	xo	LA	31.9
" "	6	Fr	12-Aug-88	Exeter	Plymouth	1V54	1325LvpPly	xo	LA	52.0
" "	7	Sa	27-May-89	Par	Newquay	1C38	1205PadNqy	xo	LA	20.8
" "	8	Sa	19-Aug-89	Par	Penzance		1025PadPnz	xo	LA	44.8
" "	9	Sa	19-Aug-89	Penzance	Exeter		1620PnzPad	xo	LA	131.6
" "	10	Th	31-Aug-89	Par	Plymouth		1630PnzPad	xo	LA	34.8
" "	11	Sa	07-Oct-89	Penzance	Plymouth		0827PnzPad	xo	LA	79.5
" "	12	Sa	07-Jul-90	Par	Penzance	1C02	2359PadPnz	xo	LA	44.0
" "	13	Th	17-Oct-96	Exeter	Plymouth	1V56	1203NclPly	xo	CF	52.0
" "	14	Sa	02-May-98	Par	Penzance	1V29	2350WloPnz	xo	CF	44.8
37675	1	Sa	20-Jun-87	Par	Plymouth	1M62	1005NqyMcp	xo	LA	34.8
" "	2	Sa	27-Aug-88	Par	Newquay	1V59	0700GgcNqy	xo	LA	20.8
" "	3	Sa	01-Apr-89	Par	Plymouth		1730PnzBtm	xo	LA	34.8

Loco	log	dy	date	from	to	code	train	detail		miles
" "	4	Sa	14-Oct-89	Plymouth	Exeter		0815PlyYrk	xo	LA	52.0
" "	5	Sa	08-Dec-90	Par	Exeter		0930PnzEdb	xo	LA	86.8
" "	6	Mo	18-Mar-91	Par	Penzance	1C76	1935PadPnz	xo	LA	44.8
" "	7	Sa	13-Jun-92	Exeter	Plymouth	1V47	1018McpPnz	xo	LA	52.0
" "	8	Su	14-Jun-92	Exeter	Plymouth	1C72	1835PadPly	xo	LA	52.0
" "	9	Sa	22-Aug-92	Par	Newquay	1V26	2355LdsNqy	xo	LA	20.8
" "	10	Sa	22-Aug-92	Newquay	Par	1M62	0815NqyMcp	xe	LA	20.8
" "	11	Tu	28-Sep-93	Largin	Plymouth		1445PnzPad	xo	LA	22.9
37679	1	Su	19-Jul-98	Exeter	Plymouth	1C82	2015PadPly	xo	IM	52.0
" "	2	Fr	14-Aug-98	Exeter	Penzance	1V50	0840GgcPnz	xo	IM	131.6
" "	3	Sa	15-Aug-98	Penzance	Bristol	1M56	0840PnzMcp	xo	IM	207.1
" "	4	Su	23-Aug-98	Exeter	Plymouth	1V42	0747McpPly	xo	IM	52.0
" "	5	Sa	29-Aug-98	Exeter	Birmingham	1M39	1844PgnBns	xo	IM	165.6
" "	6	Tu	01-Sep-98	Exeter	Plymouth	1V61	1502NclPly	xo	IM	52.0
37693	1	Fr	07-May-99	Plymouth	Bristol	1M56	0848PnzMcp	xo	TO	127.5
" "	2	Fr	14-May-99	Exeter	Penzance	1V50	0840GgcPnz	xo	TO	131.6
37694	1	Sa	16-May-87	Wolverhampton	Paignton	1V71	1020GgcPgn	xo	CF	206.8
" "	2	We	01-Dec-99	Chacewater	Truro	1A91	1530PnzPad	xo	TO	5.4
37695	1	Sa	13-Jan-96	Par	Penzance	1V29	2350WloPnz	xo	CF	44.8
" "	2	Sa	07-Aug-99	Crewe	Paignton	1V41	0810LvpPgn	xo	TO	246.6
" "	3	We	07-Aug-99	Paignton	Birmingham	1M25	1617PgnMcp	xo	TO	193.9
37696	1	We	10-Jan-96	Exeter	Penzance	1V52	0850EdbPnz	xo	CF	131.6
" "	2	Sa	08-Jun-96	Probus	Truro	1V47	1017McpPnz	xo	CF	6.0
" "	3	Fr	31-Jul-98	Exeter	Plymouth	1V61	1502NclPly	xo	CF	52.0
37698	1	Su	11-Apr-99	Torquay	Exeter	1A72	1610PgnPad	xo	TO	26.2
37699	1	Fr	19-Dec-86	Liskeard	Lostwithiel	1C11	0645SdnPnz	xo	CF	12.6
" "	2	Tu	13-Jan-87	St Austell	Penzance	1C02	2359PadPnz	xo	CF	40.2
" "	3	Tu	13-Jan-87	Penzance	Plymouth	2C83	1200PnzPly	xo	CF	79.5
37701	1	Sa	06-Jun-98	Plymouth	Bristol	1M56	0840PnzMcp	xo	CF	127.5
" "	2	Sa	06-Jun-98	Worle Junction	Exeter	1V46	1017McpPnz	xo	CF	58.7
" "	3	Su	07-Jun-98	Exeter	Plymouth	1V42	0747McpPly	xo	CF	52.0
" "	4	Su	07-Jun-98	Exeter	Plymouth	1V68	1425NclPly	xo	CF	52.0
" "	5	Sa	13-Jun-98	Paignton	Exeter	1M39	1844PgnBns	xo	CF	28.3
37706	1	Sa	28-Aug-99	Tiverton Jn	Bristol	1E33	1001PgnNcl	xo	TO	60.7
37885	1	Su	13-Sep-98	Exeter	Plymouth	1V80	1550NclPly	xo	IM	52.0
37886	1	Sa	29-Aug-92	Exeter	Bristol	1S66	1037PgnGgc	xo	CF	75.5
37887	1	Mo	29-Sep-97	Exeter	Plymouth	1C20	0935PadPly	xo	CF	52.0
37891	1	Fr	13-Nov-98	Paignton	Exeter	1E31	0821PgnNcl	xo	EH	28.3
" "	2	Su	22-Nov-98	Exeter	Plymouth	1V68	1357NclPly	xo	EH	52.0
37894	1	We	09-Jul-97	Exeter	Plymouth	1C82	2035PadPly	xo	CF	52.0
37895	1	Th	14-Nov-96	Dainton	Bristol	1S71	0722PnzEdb	xo	CF	99.6
" "	2	Mo	07-Apr-97	Exeter	Penzance	1V29	2350WloPnz	xo	CF	131.6
37897	1	Fr	27-Mar-98	Starcross	Newton Abbot	1V57	0910AbdPly	xo	CF	11.7
" "	2	Fr	14-Aug-98	Exeter	Penzance	1V50	0840GgcPnz	xo	CΓ	131.6
" "	3	Sa	15-Aug-98	Penzance	Exeter	1M56	0840PnzMcp	xo	CF	131.6
" "	4	Su	23-Aug-98	Exeter	Plymouth	1V42	0747McpPly	xo	CF	52.0
" "	5	Fr	10-Sep-98	Exeter	Plymouth	1V61	1502NclPly	xo	CF	52.0

Chapter 9 – List of pilot locos on 1C09 0635 Bristol – Plymouth

Log	Pilot	Train Loco	date	from	to	code	train
1	45012	46026	17-Aug-84	Bristol	Exeter	1C09	0635BtmPly
2	31173	50029	30-Oct-84	Bristol	Exeter	1C09	0635BtmPly
3	47195	50020	11-Jan-85	Bristol	Exeter	1C09	0635BtmPly
4	37099	50009	26-Jan-85	Bristol	Exeter	1C09	0635BtmPly
5	47463	50048	08-Feb-85	Bristol	Exeter	1C09	0635BtmPly
6	37267	50020	01-Mar-85	Bristol	Exeter	1C09	0635BtmPly
7	37182	47492	17-May-85	Bristol	Exeter	1C09	0635BtmPly
8	45069	50012	21-May-85	Bristol	Exeter	1C09	0635BtmPly
9	45070	50034	21-Jun-85	Bristol	Exeter	1C09	0635BtmPly
10	45130	47418	18-Oct-85	Bristol	Exeter	1C09	0635BtmPly
11	47246	50024	22-Oct-85	Bristol	Exeter	1C09	0635BtmPly
12	37185	50032	29-Oct-85	Bristol	Exeter	1C09	0635BtmPly
13	37158	50003	22-Nov-85	Bristol	Exeter	1C09	0635BtmPly
14	45112	47428	03-Jan-86	Bristol	Exeter	1C09	0635BtmPly
15	37235	47415	21-Jan-86	Bristol	Exeter	1C09	0635BtmPly
16	37101	50031	31-Jan-86	Bristol	Exeter	1C09	0635BtmPly
17	37078	50012	11-Feb-86	Bristol	Exeter	1C09	0635BtmPly
18	37232	47431	14-Feb-86	Bristol	Exeter	1C09	0635BtmPly
19	37204	47501	04-Mar-86	Bristol	Exeter	1C09	0635BtmPly
20	37129	50046	18-Mar-86	Bristol	Exeter	1C09	0635BtmPly
21	37232	50035	21-Mar-86	Bristol	Exeter	1C09	0635BtmPly
22	37158	50002	25-Mar-86	Bristol	Exeter	1C09	0635BtmPly
23	31159	50001	04-Apr-86	Bristol	Exeter	1C09	0635BtmPly
25	37208	50049	15-Apr-86	Bristol	Exeter	1C09	0635BtmPly
26	47590	50019	28-Apr-86	Bristol	Plymouth	1C09	0635BtmPly
27	45104	50033	04-Jul-86	Bristol	Exeter	1C09	0635BtmPly
28	47157	47588	15-Jul-86	Bristol	Exeter	1C09	0635BtmPly
29	45108	47009	01-Aug-86	Bristol	Exeter	1C09	0635BtmPly
30	47109	50015	08-Aug-86	Bristol	Exeter	1C09	0635BtmPly
31	47611	50045	12-Aug-86	Bristol	Exeter	1C09	0635BtmPly
32	47232	50013	26-Sep-86	Bristol	Exeter	1C09	0635BtmPly
33	45037	50022	30-Sep-86	Bristol	Exeter	1C09	0635BtmPly
34	31466	50013	07-Oct-86	Bristol	Exeter	1C09	0635BtmPly
35	45052	47610	10-Oct-86	Bristol	Exeter	1C09	0635BtmPly
36	45051	50013	17-Oct-86	Bristol	Exeter	1C09	0635BtmPly
37	47204	50013	21-Oct-86	Bristol	Exeter	1C09	0635BtmPly